Simple 1-2-3™
Seafood

pil

Publications International, Ltd.

Favorite Brand Name Recipes at www.fbnr.com

Pictured on the front cover: Grilled Sea Bass with Ripe Olive 'n Caper Salsa *(page 113).*
Pictured on the back cover *(clockwise from top):* Beijing Fillet of Sole *(page 134),* Tuna in Crispy Won Ton Cups *(page 6)* and Tuna Monte Cristo Sandwich *(page 37).*

ISBN-13: 978-1-4127-2578-1
ISBN-10: 1-4127-2578-X

Library of Congress Control Number: 2007921109

Manufactured in China.

8 7 6 5 4 3 2 1

Microwave Cooking: Microwave ovens vary in wattage. Use the cooking times as guidelines and check for doneness before adding more time.

Preparation/Cooking Times: Preparation times are based on the approximate amount of time required to assemble the recipe before cooking, baking, chilling or serving. These times include preparation steps such as measuring, chopping and mixing. The fact that some preparations and cooking can be done simultaneously is taken into account. Preparation of optional ingredients and serving suggestions is not included.

Contents

Soups & Starters

Asian Pasta & Shrimp Soup

1 package (3½ ounces)
  fresh shiitake
  mushrooms
2 teaspoons Asian
  sesame oil
2 cans (14½ ounces each)
  vegetable broth
4 ounces angel hair pasta,
  broken into 2-inch
  lengths (about 1 cup)
½ pound medium raw
  shrimp, peeled and
  deveined
4 ounces snow peas, cut
  into thin strips
2 tablespoons *French's®*
  Honey Dijon Mustard
1 tablespoon *Frank's®*
  RedHot® Original
  Cayenne Pepper Sauce
⅛ teaspoon ground ginger

1. Remove and discard stems from mushrooms. Cut mushrooms into thin strips. Heat oil in large saucepan over medium-high heat. Add mushrooms; stir-fry 3 minutes or just until tender.

2. Add broth and *½ cup water* to saucepan. Heat to boiling. Stir in pasta. Cook 2 minutes or just until tender.

3. Add remaining ingredients, stirring frequently. Heat to boiling. Reduce heat to medium-low. Cook 2 minutes or until shrimp turn pink and peas are tender.

Makes 4 servings

Prep Time: *10 minutes*
Cook Time: *about 10 minutes*

Tuna in Crispy Won Ton Cups

18 won ton skins, each
    3¼ inches square
**Butter or olive oil
    cooking spray**
1 (3-ounce) STARKIST
    **Flavor Fresh Pouch®
    Tuna (Albacore or
    Chunk Light)**
⅓ **cup cold cooked orzo
    (rice-shaped pasta) or
    cooked rice**
¼ **cup southwestern ranch-
    style vegetable dip
    with jalapeños or other
    sour cream dip**
¼ **cup drained pimiento-
    stuffed green olives,
    chopped**
3 **tablespoons sweet pickle
    relish, drained
    Paprika, for garnish
    Chopped fresh parsley,
    for garnish**

1. Cut won tons into circles with 3-inch round cookie cutter. Spray miniature muffin pans with cooking spray. Place one circle in each muffin cup; press to sides to mold won ton to cup. Spray each won ton with cooking spray. Bake in 350°F oven 6 to 8 minutes or until golden brown; set aside.

2. In small bowl, gently mix tuna, orzo, dip, olives and relish. Refrigerate filling until ready to serve. Remove won ton cups from muffin pan. Use rounded teaspoon to fill each cup; garnish with paprika and parsley.

Makes 18 servings

Tip: Cups may be made a day ahead; store in airtight container. Reheat in 350°F oven 1 to 2 minutes to recrisp.

Prep Time: *20 minutes*

Soups & Starters

Individual Smoked Salmon Pizzas

1. Preheat oven to 425°F.

2. Divide bread dough into 6 equal pieces. Pat each dough piece into a ball and place on lightly floured surface. Roll out each dough piece into 6- or 7-inch round with rolling pin on lightly floured surface. Transfer dough pieces to 2 baking sheets.

3. Sprinkle cheese over dough pieces. Arrange onion and tomatoes over cheese; sprinkle lightly with salt and pepper. Bake 12 minutes or until crust is golden brown. Top each pizza with smoked salmon, sour cream, capers and dill. Serve warm or at room temperature.

Makes 6 servings

1 loaf (16 ounces) frozen white bread dough, thawed

3 cups (12 ounces) shredded mozzarella cheese

1 small red onion, cut crosswise into rings

2 ripe tomatoes, cut crosswise into thin slices

Salt and black pepper to taste

8 ounces thinly sliced smoked salmon or lox, cut into strips

Sour cream

Capers and fresh dill sprigs

Potato-Crab Chowder

1 package (10 ounces) frozen corn, thawed
1 cup frozen hash brown potatoes, thawed
¾ cup finely chopped carrots
1 teaspoon dried thyme
¾ teaspoon garlic-pepper seasoning
3 cups fat-free reduced-sodium chicken broth
½ cup water
1 cup evaporated milk
3 tablespoons cornstarch
1 can (6 ounces) crabmeat, drained
½ cup sliced green onions

Slow Cooker Directions

1. Place corn, potatoes and carrots in slow cooker. Sprinkle with thyme and garlic-pepper. Add broth and water.

2. Cover; cook on LOW 3½ to 4½ hours.

3. Blend evaporated milk and cornstarch until smooth. Stir into slow cooker. Cover; cook on HIGH 15 to 30 minutes. Just before serving, stir in crabmeat and green onions until heated through. *Makes 5 servings*

Soups & Starters

Seafood Spread

1. Beat cream cheese in medium bowl with electric mixer at medium speed until smooth. Add whitefish, green onion, dill, lemon juice and pepper; mix until well blended. Refrigerate until ready to serve.

2. Serve with rye bread slices and garnish with lime wedges, if desired.

Makes 12 servings

Prep Time: *10 minutes plus refrigerating*

1 package (8 ounces) cream cheese, softened
½ pound smoked whitefish, skinned, boned and flaked
2 tablespoons minced green onion
1 tablespoon plus 1 teaspoon chopped fresh dill
1 teaspoon lemon juice
¼ teaspoon black pepper
Rye bread halves
Lime wedges, for garnish (optional)

Soups & Starters

Cool Shrimp Spring Rolls with Wasabi Soy Dipping Sauce

1 cup *French's*®
  Gourmayo™ Wasabi
  Horseradish Light
  Mayonnaise
2 tablespoons reduced-
  sodium soy sauce
2 tablespoons lemon juice
1 tablespoon grated peeled
  fresh ginger
1 tablespoon minced green
  onion
4 cups shredded cabbage
  mix
12 (9-inch) rice paper
  wrappers, soaked in
  cold water until
  softened
36 shelled cooked medium
  shrimp (about
  ½ pound)
6 cups shredded Iceberg or
  Romaine lettuce

1. Prepare Wasabi Soy Dipping Sauce: Combine mayonnaise, soy sauce, lemon juice, ginger and green onion in measuring cup. Pour ¾ cup sauce into medium bowl; add cabbage and toss to combine. Cover and chill remaining sauce.

2. Place 1 rice paper wrapper on work surface. Arrange 3 shrimp across center of wrapper. Top with about 2 tablespoons cabbage mixture and ½ cup shredded lettuce. Fold sides of wrapper in, then roll up. Repeat with remaining wrappers and ingredients.

3. To serve: Arrange 2 spring rolls on lettuce-lined serving plate. Garnish with peanuts and green onions, if desired. Serve with remaining Wasabi Soy Dipping Sauce. *Makes 6 servings*

Tip: Rice paper wrappers are available in Asian grocery markets and gourmet specialty stores.

Tip: Wasabi Soy Dipping Sauce can be used with egg rolls, pot stickers and wontons.

Prep Time: *30 minutes*

Steamed Clams in Wine Broth

Bring margarine, wine, water, parsley and hot pepper sauce to a boil in bottom of steamer. Arrange clams on steamer rack and place in steamer. Cover. Steam about 8 minutes or until clams open. Discard any clams that do not open. Divide clams into 3 or 4 serving bowls. Ladle broth over them.

Makes 3 to 4 servings

Favorite recipe from **National Fisheries Institute**

6 tablespoons margarine, melted
¾ cup dry white wine
¾ cup water
1½ tablespoons chopped fresh parsley
¼ teaspoon hot pepper sauce
4 pounds cherrystone or little neck clams, scrubbed

Smoked Salmon Roses

1 package (8 ounces)
   cream cheese, softened
1 tablespoon prepared
   horseradish
1 tablespoon minced fresh
   dill plus whole sprigs
1 tablespoon half-and-half
16 slices (12 to 16 ounces)
   smoked salmon
1 red bell pepper, cut into
   thin strips

1. Combine cream cheese, horseradish, minced dill and half-and-half in small bowl. Beat until light and creamy.

2. Spread 1 tablespoon cream cheese mixture over each salmon slice. Roll up jelly-roll fashion. Slice each roll in half crosswise. Arrange salmon rolls, cut sides down, on serving dish to resemble roses. Garnish each "rose" by tucking 1 pepper strip and 1 dill sprig into center. *Makes 32 servings*

Crab and Artichoke Stuffed Mushrooms

Remove any pieces of shell or cartilage from crabmeat. Combine crabmeat, artichoke hearts, mayonnaise, Parmesan cheese and seasonings; mix until well blended. Remove stems from mushrooms and fill the caps with crabmeat mixture. Place in a lightly greased, shallow baking dish. Bake in a preheated 400°F oven for 10 minutes or until hot and bubbly.

Makes 30 appetizer servings

Favorite recipe from **Florida Department of Agriculture and Consumer Services, Bureau of Seafood and Aquaculture**

½ pound Florida blue crab meat
1 (14-ounce) can artichoke hearts, drained and finely chopped
1 cup mayonnaise*
½ cup grated Parmesan cheese
¼ teaspoon lemon pepper seasoning
⅛ teaspoon salt
⅛ teaspoon cayenne pepper
30 large fresh Florida mushrooms

*Or, you can substitute mixture of ½ cup mayonnaise and ½ cup plain yogurt.

Cioppino

2 tablespoons olive or vegetable oil
1½ cups chopped onion
1 cup chopped celery
½ cup chopped green bell pepper
1 clove garlic, minced
1 can (28 ounces) CONTADINA® Recipe Ready Crushed Tomatoes
1 can (6 ounces) CONTADINA Tomato Paste
1 teaspoon Italian herb seasoning
1 teaspoon salt
½ teaspoon ground black pepper
2 cups water
1 cup dry red wine or chicken broth
3 pounds white fish, shrimp, scallops, cooked crab, cooked lobster, clams and/or oysters (in any proportion)

1. Heat oil in large saucepan. Add onion, celery, bell pepper and garlic; sauté until vegetables are tender. Add tomatoes, tomato paste, Italian seasoning, salt, black pepper, water and wine.

2. Bring to a boil. Reduce heat to low; simmer, uncovered, for 15 minutes.

3. To prepare fish and seafood: scrub clams and oysters under running water. Place in ½-inch boiling water in separate large saucepan; cover. Bring to a boil. Reduce heat to low; simmer just until shells open, about 3 minutes. Set aside.

4. Cut crab, lobster, fish and scallops into bite-size pieces.

5. Shell and devein shrimp. Add fish to tomato mixture; simmer 5 minutes. Add scallops and shrimp; simmer 5 minutes.

6. Add crab, lobster and reserved clams and oysters; simmer until heated through.   *Makes about 14 cups*

Prep Time: 30 minutes
Cook Time: 35 minutes

Hot or Cold Tuna Snacks

1. Combine tuna, cream cheese, parsley, onion, oregano and pepper in medium bowl; mix well. Mound about 1 tablespoon tuna mixture on top of each cucumber slice.

2. To serve cold, place on serving plate and garnish with capers.

3. To serve hot, preheat oven to 450°F. Spray baking sheet with nonstick cooking spray. Place snacks on prepared baking sheet; bake about 10 minutes or until tops are puffed and brown. Transfer to serving plate and garnish with capers.

Makes 6 servings

Note: Capers are the flower buds of a bush native to the Mediterranean and parts of India. The buds are picked, sun-dried, then pickled. Capers should be rinsed before using to remove excess salt.

1 can (6 ounces) chunk light tuna packed in water, well drained
4 ounces cream cheese
1 tablespoon chopped fresh parsley
1 tablespoon minced onion
½ teaspoon dried oregano
½ teaspoon black pepper
18 (½-inch-thick) slices seedless cucumber
Capers for garnish

Apricot BBQ Glazed Shrimp and Bacon

1 can (8 ounces) sliced water chestnuts, drained

36 medium raw shrimp, peeled and deveined (about 1¼ pounds)

9 bacon slices, each cut into 4 pieces

⅓ cup apricot fruit spread

⅓ cup barbecue sauce

1 tablespoon grated fresh ginger

1 tablespoon cider vinegar

⅛ teaspoon red pepper flakes

1. Place 1 water chestnut slice on top of each shrimp. Wrap 1 piece of bacon around shrimp and secure with wooden toothpick. Repeat with remaining water chestnuts, shrimp and bacon.

2. Preheat broiler. Line broiler pan with foil; insert broiler rack. Coat broiler rack with nonstick cooking spray. Place wrapped shrimp on rack.

3. Combine fruit spread, barbecue sauce, ginger, vinegar and red pepper flakes in small bowl. Brush sauce evenly over shrimp. Broil 3 minutes; turn. Baste and broil 3 minutes more; turn again. Baste and broil 2 minute more or until edges of bacon begin to brown. *Makes 36 appetizers*

Creamy Crab Chowder

1. Melt butter over medium heat in Dutch oven. Add onion and garlic. Cook and stir 6 minutes or until softened but not browned. Add celery and bell peppers. Cook 8 minutes or until celery is tender, stirring often.

2. Add broth and potatoes. Bring to a boil over high heat. Reduce heat to low and simmer 20 minutes. Add corn; cook 5 minutes or until potatoes are tender.

3. Drain crabmeat and place in small bowl. Flake to break up large pieces; add to Dutch oven. Stir in half-and-half and black pepper. Bring to a simmer. *Do not boil.* Serve hot.   *Makes 6 to 8 servings*

1 tablespoon butter
1 cup finely chopped onion
2 cloves garlic, minced
1 cup finely chopped celery
½ cup finely chopped green bell pepper
½ cup finely chopped red bell pepper
3 cans (about 14 ounces each) chicken broth
3 cups diced peeled potatoes
1 package (10 ounces) frozen corn
2 cans (6½ ounces each) lump crabmeat
½ cup half-and-half
¼ teaspoon black pepper

Salmon Celery Trees

1 can (6 ounces) pink salmon
1 tablespoon minced green onion (optional)
2 tablespoons minced fresh dill
1 tablespoon fresh lemon juice
6 ounces cream cheese, softened
Salt and black pepper
12 celery stalks
Fresh dill sprigs, 3 to 4 inches long

1. Combine salmon, green onion, if desired, dill and lemon juice in medium bowl. Mix until well combined. Add cream cheese and mash with fork until mixture is smooth. Season to taste with salt and pepper.

2. Stack celery stalks in pairs. Cut each pair into 3-inch pieces.

3. Spread 2 tablespoons salmon mixture into hollowed section of each celery piece with small spoon or knife. Press dill springs into one half of each celery pair before pressing filled sides together. Stand upright on serving platter with dill sprigs on top to resemble trees with branches. *Makes 12 servings*

Brandy-Soaked Scallops

1. Wrap one piece bacon around each scallop; secure with toothpick, if necessary. Place wrapped scallops in glass or ceramic 13×9-inch baking dish.

2. Combine brandy, oil, parsley, garlic, pepper, salt and onion powder in small bowl; mix well. Pour mixture over scallops; cover and marinate in refrigerator at least 4 hours.

3. Remove scallops from marinade; discard marinade. Arrange scallops on rack of broiler pan. Broil 4 inches from heat 7 to 10 minutes or until bacon is browned. Turn; broil 5 minutes more or until scallops are opaque. Remove toothpicks. *Makes 8 servings*

1 pound bacon, cut in half crosswise
2 pounds sea scallops
½ cup brandy
⅓ cup olive oil
2 tablespoons chopped fresh parsley
1 clove garlic, minced
1 teaspoon black pepper
½ teaspoon salt
½ teaspoon onion powder

Maryland Crab Cakes

1 pound fresh crabmeat, cartilage removed
10 crackers (2 inches each), crushed (½ cup crumbs)
1 stalk celery, finely chopped
1 green onion, finely chopped
1 egg
3 tablespoons tartar sauce
1 teaspoon seafood seasoning
  Nonstick cooking spray
2 teaspoons vegetable oil
  Lemon wedges or slices (optional)

1. Combine crabmeat, cracker crumbs, celery and green onion in medium bowl; set aside.

2. Mix egg, tartar sauce and seafood seasoning in small bowl; pour over crabmeat mixture. Gently mix so large lumps will not be broken. Shape into 6 (¾-inch-thick) patties. Cover; refrigerate 30 minutes.

3. Spray large skillet with cooking spray. Add oil; heat over medium-high heat. Place crab cakes in skillet; cook 3 to 4 minutes on each side or until cakes are lightly browned. Garnish with lemon wedges or slices, if desired.

Makes 6 servings

Spicy Thai Shrimp Soup

1. Heat wok over medium-high heat 1 minute or until hot. Add oil to wok; heat 30 seconds. Add shrimp and jalapeño; stir-fry 1 minute. Add paprika and ground red pepper. Stir-fry 1 minute more or until shrimp turn pink and opaque. Remove shrimp mixture to bowl; set aside.

2. Add shrimp shells to wok and stir-fry 30 seconds. Add chicken broth and lemon and lime peels; bring to a boil. Cover; reduce heat to low. Simmer 15 minutes.

3. Remove shells and peels from broth with slotted spoon; discard. Add mushrooms and shrimp mixture to broth; bring to a boil. Stir in lemon and lime juices, soy sauce and chili pepper strips. Ladle soup into bowls. Sprinkle with cilantro. Serve immediately. *Makes 8 first-course servings*

1 tablespoon vegetable oil
1 pound medium raw shrimp, peeled and deveined, shells reserved
1 jalapeño pepper,* sliced
1 tablespoon paprika
¼ teaspoon ground red pepper
4 cans (14½ ounces each) chicken broth
1 (½-inch) strip *each* lemon and lime peel
1 can (15 ounces) straw mushrooms, drained
Juice of 1 lemon
Juice of 1 lime
2 tablespoons soy sauce
1 fresh red Thai chili pepper* *or* ¼ small red bell pepper, cut into thin strips
¼ cup fresh cilantro

Jalapeño and other chili peppers can sting and irritate the skin, so wear rubber gloves when handling peppers and do not touch your eyes.

1 cup cottage cheese
1 tablespoon mayonnaise
1 tablespoon lemon juice
2 teaspoons dry ranch-style salad dressing mix
1 can (3 ounces) chunk white tuna packed in water, drained and flaked
2 tablespoons sliced green onion or chopped celery
1 teaspoon dried parsley
1 package (12 ounces) peeled baby carrots

Swimming Tuna Dip

1. Combine cottage cheese, mayonnaise, lemon juice and salad dressing mix in blender or food processor. Cover and blend until smooth.

2. Combine tuna, green onion and parsley in small bowl. Stir in cottage cheese mixture. Serve with carrots. *Makes 4 servings*

Crabmeat Crostini

Remove any remaining shell particles from crab meat. Combine all ingredients except bread, mix well, cover and refrigerate for one hour. Arrange bread slices on baking sheet and place equal portions of crab mixture on each slice. Broil 4 to 6 inches from source of heat for 6 to 8 minutes or until cheese melts or begins to brown.   *Makes 12 appetizer servings*

*Favorite recipe from **Florida Department of Agriculture and Consumer Services, Bureau of Seafood and Aquaculture***

1 **pound Florida blue crab or stone crab meat**
1½ **cups shredded low-fat mozzarella cheese**
½ **cup Florida pecan pieces, toasted and chopped**
2 **Florida datil peppers, seeded and chopped (or other hot peppers)**
2 **teaspoons chopped fresh Florida rosemary leaves**
2 **teaspoons chopped fresh Florida thyme leaves**
1 **(3-ounce) package sun dried tomatoes, rehydrated and chopped**
12 **(1-inch-thick) slices French bread, sliced diagonally**

New England Fish Chowder

¼ pound bacon, diced
1 cup chopped onion
½ cup chopped celery
2 cups diced russet
    potatoes
2 tablespoons all-purpose
    flour
2 cups water
1 bay leaf
1 teaspoon dried dill weed
1 teaspoon salt
½ teaspoon dried thyme
½ teaspoon black pepper
1 pound cod, haddock or
    halibut fillets, skinned,
    boned and cut into
    1-inch pieces
2 cups milk
    Chopped fresh parsley
    (optional)

1. Cook bacon in 5-quart Dutch oven over medium-high heat, stirring occasionally. Remove bacon with slotted spoon; drain on paper towels. Add onion and celery to drippings. Cook and stir until onion is soft. Stir in potatoes; cook 1 minute. Stir in flour; cook 1 minute more.

2. Add water, bay leaf, dill, salt, thyme and pepper. Bring to a boil over high heat. Reduce heat to low. Cover and simmer 25 minutes or until potatoes are fork-tender. Add fish; simmer, covered, 5 minutes or until fish begins to flake when tested with fork. Discard bay leaf. Add milk; heat through. Do not boil. Return bacon to chowder. Ladle into soup bowls. Garnish with parsley, if desired. *Makes 4 to 6 servings*

Salmon & Brie Pizza

1. In a medium bowl, mix flour, ⅓ cup oil and 1 tablespoon dill. Gradually add water, stirring until well combined and dough is formed. (Dough will be wet; do not add more flour.) Knead dough in the bowl with your hands for 4 minutes.

2. Form dough into a ball. Pinch off 8 (1-inch) balls of dough. With a rolling pin, roll each ball into a 4-inch circle.

3. Heat remaining 2 tablespoons oil in a small skillet over medium heat. Fry dough circles for about 20 seconds on each side, or until lightly browned; remove from skillet, and drain on paper towels. Repeat with remaining dough.

4. Cut brie into 16 slices. Place 2 slices on each crust. Top with 2 slices salmon. Sprinkle with remaining 2 tablespoons dill, capers and onion.

Makes 8 servings

Variation: Preheat broiler. Layer salmon on prepared pizza crust and top with brie, dill, capers and onion. Place on broiler pan and broil just until cheese is melted.

1 cup all-purpose flour
⅓ cup plus 2 tablespoons canola oil, divided
3 tablespoons fresh dill, divided
¼ cup water
8 ounces brie cheese
8 ounces smoked salmon
1 tablespoon capers
3 tablespoons chopped red onion

Spicy Ale Shrimp

3 bottles (12 ounces each) pilsner beer, divided
1 tablespoon seafood boil seasoning blend
1 teaspoon mustard seeds
1 teaspoon red pepper flakes
1 lemon, sliced into quarters
1 pound large raw shrimp (15 to 20 count), peeled and deveined, tails intact
Dipping Sauce (recipe follows)

1. Pour one bottle of beer into large bowl half-filled with ice; set aside.

2. Add remaining 2 bottles of beer, seafood boil seasoning, mustard seeds and red pepper flakes into 1-gallon stockpot. Squeeze lemon juice into pot, add lemon quarters. Bring beer mixture to simmer over medium-high heat.

3. Add shrimp. Cover; remove from heat. Let sit 3 minutes to cook shrimp. Drain; transfer shrimp to bowl of chilled beer and ice cubes. When cool, remove shrimp from bowl; arrange on platter. Serve with Dipping Sauce.

Makes 15 to 20 shrimp

Dipping Sauce

1 cup ketchup
1 tablespoon grated fresh horseradish
1 tablespoon chili-garlic paste
Juice of one lime
Hot pepper sauce

Combine ketchup, horseradish, chili-garlic paste and lime juice in small glass bowl. Add hot pepper sauce to taste; mix well. Cover; refrigerate 1 hour.

Makes about 1 cup sauce

Soups & Starters

Blue Crab Stuffed Tomatoes

Remove any shell or cartilage from crabmeat.

Cut tomatoes in half lengthwise. Carefully scoop out centers of tomatoes; discard pulp. Invert on paper towels.

Combine crabmeat, celery, yogurt, onion, bell pepper, lemon juice, salt and black pepper. Mix well.

Fill tomato halves with crab mixture. Refrigerate 2 hours.

Makes 20 appetizers

Favorite recipe from **Florida Department of Agriculture and Consumer Services, Bureau of Seafood and Aquaculture**

½ **pound Florida blue crabmeat**
10 **plum tomatoes**
½ **cup finely chopped celery**
⅓ **cup plain low-fat yogurt**
2 **tablespoons minced green onion**
2 **tablespoons finely chopped red bell pepper**
½ **teaspoon lemon juice**
¼ **teaspoon salt**
⅛ **teaspoon black pepper**

Seafood Stew

2 tablespoons butter
1 cup chopped onion
1 cup green bell pepper
  strips
1 teaspoon dried dill weed
  Dash ground red pepper
1 can (about 14 ounces)
  diced tomatoes
½ cup white wine
2 tablespoons lime juice
8 ounces swordfish steak,
  cut into 1-inch cubes
8 ounces bay or sea
  scallops, cut into
  quarters
1 bottle (8 ounces) clam
  juice
2 tablespoons cornstarch
2 cups frozen diced
  potatoes, thawed and
  drained
8 ounces frozen medium
  cooked shrimp, thawed
  and drained
½ cup whipping cream

1. Melt butter in Dutch oven over medium-high heat. Add onion, bell pepper, dill weed and ground red pepper; cook and stir 5 minutes or until vegetables are tender.

2. Reduce heat to medium. Add tomatoes with juice, wine and lime juice; bring to a boil. Add swordfish and scallops; cook and stir 2 minutes.

3. Combine clam juice and cornstarch in small bowl; stir until smooth.

4. Increase heat to high. Add potatoes, shrimp, whipping cream and clam juice mixture; bring to a boil. Season to taste with salt and black pepper.

Makes 6 servings

Prep and Cook Time: *20 minutes*

Oysters Romano

1. Preheat oven to 375°F. Place shells with oysters on baking sheet. Top each oyster with 1 piece bacon. Bake 10 minutes or until bacon is crisp.

2. Meanwhile, combine bread crumbs, butter and garlic salt in small bowl. Spoon mixture over oysters; sprinkle with cheese. Bake 5 to 10 minutes or until cheese melts. Garnish with chives.

Makes 12 appetizers

12 oysters, shucked and on the half shell
2 slices bacon, cut into 12 pieces
½ cup Italian seasoned dry bread crumbs
2 tablespoons butter or margarine, melted
½ teaspoon garlic salt
6 tablespoons grated Romano or Parmesan cheese
Fresh chives (optional)

Coconut Shrimp with Pear Chutney

1. Preheat oven to 425°F. Spray baking sheet with nonstick cooking spray. Prepare Pear Chutney.

2. Meanwhile, melt butter in skillet. Remove from heat. Add shrimp and coat with butter. Combine coconut, curry powder and salt in shallow bowl. Press shrimp into coconut mixture to coat all sides. Place shrimp on prepared baking sheet. Bake 4 minutes. Turn shrimp over and bake another 2 minutes or until shrimp are pink and opaque. Serve with Pear Chutney.   *Makes 4 servings*

Pear Chutney

Pear Chutney (recipe follows)
3 tablespoons unsalted butter
1 pound large raw shrimp, peeled and deveined
½ cup shredded unsweetened coconut
¾ teaspoon curry powder
½ teaspoon salt

1 tablespoon vegetable oil
1 jalapeño pepper, seeded and minced
1 small shallot, minced
1½ teaspoons grated fresh ginger
1 medium unpeeled ripe pear, cored and diced into ½-inch pieces
1 tablespoon cider vinegar
1 teaspoon brown sugar
⅛ teaspoon salt
1 tablespoon chopped green onion

Heat oil in medium saucepan. Add jalapeño, shallot and ginger. Cook over low heat 5 minutes or until shallot is tender. Add pear, vinegar, brown sugar and salt. Stir in 1 tablespoon water. Cover; cook over low heat 15 minutes or until pear is tender, adding more water if mixture becomes dry. Stir in green onion; cook 1 minute to soften.   *Makes 2 cups*

Southern Crab Cakes with Rémoulade Dipping Sauce

1. To prepare dipping sauce, combine ¼ cup mayonnaise, 1 tablespoon mustard and ¼ teaspoon hot pepper sauce in small bowl; mix well. Refrigerate until ready to serve.

2. Preheat oven to 200°F. Pick out and discard any shell or cartilage from crabmeat. Combine crabmeat, ¾ cup bread crumbs and green onions in medium bowl. Add remaining ¼ cup mayonnaise, egg white, remaining 1 tablespoon mustard and remaining ½ teaspoon pepper sauce; mix well. Using ¼ cup mixture per cake, shape into 8 (½-inch-thick) cakes. Roll crab cakes lightly in remaining ¾ cup bread crumbs.

3. Heat large nonstick skillet over medium heat; add 1 teaspoon oil. Add 4 crab cakes; cook 4 to 5 minutes per side or until golden brown. Transfer to serving platter; keep warm in oven. Repeat with remaining 1 teaspoon oil and crab cakes. Serve crab cakes warm with lemon wedges and dipping sauce.

Makes 8 servings

½ cup mayonnaise, divided
2 tablespoons coarse grain or spicy brown mustard, divided
¾ teaspoon hot pepper sauce, divided
10 ounces fresh lump crabmeat
1½ cups fresh white or sourdough bread crumbs, divided
¼ cup chopped green onions
1 egg white, lightly beaten
2 teaspoons olive oil, divided
Lemon wedges

Salmon, Corn & Barley Chowder

1 teaspoon canola oil
¼ cup chopped onion
1 clove garlic, minced
2½ cups chicken broth
¼ cup quick-cooking barley
1 tablespoon water
1 tablespoon all-purpose flour
1 can (4 ounces) salmon, drained
1 cup frozen corn, thawed
⅓ cup milk
½ teaspoon chili powder
¼ teaspoon ground cumin
¼ teaspoon dried oregano
⅛ teaspoon salt
1 tablespoon minced fresh cilantro
⅛ teaspoon black pepper

1. Heat oil in medium saucepan over medium heat. Add onion and garlic. Cook and stir 1 to 2 minutes or until onion is tender.

2. Add broth; bring to a boil. Stir in barley. Cover; reduce heat and simmer 10 minutes or until barley is tender.

3. Stir water slowly into flour in cup until smooth; set aside. Remove and discard bones and skin from salmon; flake salmon into bite-size pieces.

4. Add salmon, corn and milk to saucepan; stir until combined. Stir in flour mixture, then chili powder, cumin, oregano and salt. Simmer gently 2 to 3 minutes or until slightly thickened. Stir in cilantro and black pepper. Serve with lime wedges, if desired. *Makes 2 servings*

Mini Tuna Tarts

Combine tuna, mayonnaise, pickle relish, onion and cheese; mix well. Add salt and pepper. Separate each biscuit into 2 halves. Press each half in bottom of lightly greased muffin pan to form a cup. Spoon scant tablespoon tuna mixture into each muffin cup. Bake in preheated 400°F oven 8 to 10 minutes or until edges of biscuits are just golden. Serve hot or cold. *Makes 20 servings*

Prep Time: *15 minutes*

1 (3-ounce) STARKIST Flavor Fresh Pouch® Tuna (Albacore or Chunk Light)

2 tablespoons mayonnaise

2 tablespoons sweet pickle relish

1 green onion, including top, minced

¾ cup shredded Monterey Jack cheese

Salt and pepper to taste

1 package (10 count) refrigerated flaky biscuits

Soups & Starters

Sandwiches & Salads

Blazing Catfish Po' Boys

1½ pounds catfish fillets
¾ cup yellow cornmeal
1 egg
⅓ cup *Frank's® RedHot®* Original Cayenne Pepper Sauce
6 sandwich rolls, split in half
Spicy Tartar Sauce (recipe follows)
3 cups deli coleslaw

1. Cut fillets crosswise into 1-inch-wide strips. Combine cornmeal and *½ teaspoon salt* on sheet of waxed paper. Beat egg with *Frank's RedHot* Sauce in medium bowl. Dip fish pieces in egg mixture; shake off excess. Thoroughly coat with cornmeal mixture.

2. Heat *1½ cups vegetable oil* in large deep skillet or electric fryer until hot (360°F). Cook fish, in batches, 5 minutes or until cooked through and golden on all sides, turning once. Drain on paper towels.

3. Hollow out rolls if necessary. Spread bottom of each roll with about *2 tablespoons* Spicy Tartar Sauce. Layer with *½ cup* coleslaw and a few pieces of fish. Cover with top of roll. *Makes 6 sandwiches*

Spicy Tartar Sauce: Combine ⅔ cup prepared tartar sauce with ¼ cup *Frank's RedHot* Sauce.

Tip: Add flavor to your sandwich! Mix *Frank's RedHot* Sauce with mayonnaise and spread on roast beef or corned beef sandwiches.

Prep Time: *15 minutes*
Cook Time: *5 minutes*

Salmon Salad with Basil Vinaigrette

Basil Vinaigrette
- 3 tablespoons olive oil
- 1 tablespoon white wine vinegar
- 1 tablespoon minced fresh basil
- 1 clove garlic, minced
- 1 teaspoon minced fresh chives
- Salt and black pepper

Salad
- 1¼ teaspoons salt, divided
- 1 pound asparagus, trimmed
- 1 pound salmon fillets
- 1½ teaspoons olive oil
- ¼ teaspoon black pepper
- 4 lemon wedges

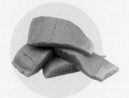

1. For Basil Vinaigrette, whisk olive oil, vinegar, basil, garlic, chives, salt and pepper to combine; set aside.

2. Preheat oven to 400°F or preheat grill to medium-hot. Place 3 inches of water and 1 teaspoon salt in large saucepan or Dutch oven. Bring to boil over high heat. Add asparagus; boil gently 6 to 8 minutes or until asparagus is crisp-tender; drain and set aside.

3. Brush salmon with olive oil. Sprinkle with remaining ¼ teaspoon salt and pepper. Place fish in shallow baking pan; cook 11 to 13 minutes or until fish just begins to flake when tested with a fork. (Or, grill on well-oiled grid over medium-hot coals 4 or 5 minutes per side or until fish just begins to flake when tested with a fork.)

4. Remove skin from salmon. Break salmon into bite-size pieces. Arrange salmon over asparagus spears on serving plate. Spoon Basil Vinaigrette over salmon. Serve with lemon wedges. *Makes 4 servings*

Tuna Monte Cristo Sandwiches

1. Place 1 slice cheese on each of 2 bread slices. Spread tuna salad evenly over 2 slices of cheese. Top each with remaining cheese and bread slices.

2. Combine milk and egg in shallow bowl; stir until well blended. Dip sandwiches in egg mixture, turning to coat well.

3. Melt butter in large nonstick skillet over medium heat. Add sandwiches; cook 4 to 5 minutes per side or until cheese melts and sandwiches are golden brown.

Makes 2 servings

Serving Suggestion: Serve with a chilled fruit salad.

Prep and Cook Time: *20 minutes*

4 slices (½ ounce each)
   Cheddar cheese
4 oval slices sourdough or
   challah (egg) bread
½ pound deli tuna salad
¼ cup milk
1 egg, beaten
2 tablespoons butter

Sandwiches & Salads

Mediterranean Shrimp and Feta Spring Salad

1 pound large raw shrimp, shells intact

1 teaspoon salt

4 cups (6 ounces) baby spinach

2 large plum tomatoes, cored and chopped

2 ounces feta cheese, crumbled

¼ cup chopped green onions

¼ cup coarsely chopped pitted kalamata olives

1 tablespoon minced fresh oregano or basil

3 tablespoons olive oil

1 tablespoon red wine vinegar

1 tablespoon small capers

½ teaspoon black pepper

1. Place shrimp in large saucepan with 1 quart of water. Add salt; bring to simmer over medium-high heat. Simmer 8 to 10 minutes or until shrimp are pink and opaque. Drain and set aside until cool enough to handle. Peel shrimp, leaving tails intact.

2. Place shrimp in large salad bowl. Add spinach, tomatoes, feta, green onions, olives and oregano. Combine olive oil, vinegar, capers and pepper in small bowl; mix well. Pour over salad and toss gently. *Makes 4 servings*

Southwest Tuna Sandwiches

1. Combine tuna, chiles, mayonnaise, cucumber, bell pepper, green onions, cilantro, cumin and garlic powder in medium bowl. Toss to mix. Break up large chunks of tuna; do not flake finely. Add salt and black pepper to taste. Cover and refrigerate 1 hour or until chilled.

2. Cut each pita in half crosswise and fill with tuna salad. Add lettuce, olives, tomatoes and Cheddar cheese to each pita half and serve. *Makes 4 servings*

2 cans (6 ounces each) tuna packed in water, drained
1 can (4 ounces) chopped mild green chiles
½ cup mayonnaise
½ cup finely chopped seeded peeled cucumber
½ cup chopped red bell pepper
¼ cup chopped green onions
¼ cup finely chopped fresh cilantro
½ teaspoon ground cumin
¼ teaspoon garlic powder
Salt and black pepper to taste
4 (6-inch) rounds pita bread
1 cup shredded leaf lettuce
½ cup sliced pitted black olives
½ cup chopped tomatoes
½ cup (2 ounces) shredded Cheddar cheese

Orange Scallops with Spinach and Walnuts

12 sea scallops (about ¾ pound)
½ cup freshly squeezed orange juice
2 tablespoons olive oil
2 packages (8 ounces each) fresh baby spinach washed, stems removed
2 tablespoons toasted walnuts
Salt and white pepper to taste
½ (11-ounce) can mandarin oranges in juice, drained

1. Rinse sea scallops and slice in half. Place in nonreactive dish and add orange juice. Stir well and set aside.

2. Place a 12-inch skillet over medium heat and add oil. Add spinach and cook until heated through and just wilted, stirring often.

3. Push spinach to edges of pan, forming a ring. Increase heat to medium high. Place scallops in the center of pan and cook scallops, turning once, 1 to 2 minutes or until opaque.

4. Add walnuts, and season with salt and white pepper. To serve, make a bed of spinach on plate; top with scallops, mandarin orange segments, walnuts and pan juices.   *Makes 4 servings*

Sandwiches & Salads

Easy Salmon Burgers with Honey Barbecue Sauce

In small bowl, combine honey, ketchup, vinegar, horseradish, garlic and red pepper flakes until well blended. Set aside half of sauce. In separate bowl, mix together salmon, bread crumbs, onion, green pepper and egg white. Blend in 2 tablespoons remaining sauce. Divide salmon mixture into 2 patties, ½ to ¾ inch thick. Place patties on well-oiled grill, 4 to 6 inches from hot coals. Grill, turning 2 to 3 times and basting with remaining sauce, until burgers are browned and cooked through. (Or place patties on lightly greased baking sheet. Broil 4 to 6 inches from heat source, turning 2 to 3 times and basting with remaining sauce, until cooked through.) Place on hamburger buns and serve with reserved sauce. *Makes 2 servings*

Favorite recipe from **National Honey Board**

⅓ cup honey
⅓ cup ketchup
1½ teaspoons cider vinegar
1 teaspoon prepared horseradish
¼ teaspoon minced garlic
⅛ teaspoon red pepper flakes (optional)
1 can (7½ ounces) salmon, drained
½ cup dried bread crumbs
¼ cup chopped onion
3 tablespoons chopped green bell pepper
1 egg white
2 hamburger buns, toasted

5 cups torn romaine
   lettuce
2 cups coarsely shredded
   red cabbage
2 medium yellow or green
   bell peppers, cut into
   strips
1½ cups sliced zucchini
1 teaspoon onion powder
½ teaspoon garlic powder
½ teaspoon black pepper
½ teaspoon ground red
   pepper
½ teaspoon dried thyme
¾ pound fresh or thawed
   frozen tuna steaks, cut
   1 inch thick
⅓ cup water
¾ cup sliced onion
2 tablespoons balsamic
   vinegar
1½ teaspoons Dijon mustard
1 teaspoon canola or
   vegetable oil
½ teaspoon chicken
   bouillon granules

Warm Blackened Tuna Salad

1. Preheat broiler. Spray broiler pan with nonstick cooking spray. Combine romaine, cabbage, bell peppers and zucchini in large bowl; set aside.

2. Combine onion powder, garlic powder, black pepper, ground red pepper and thyme in small bowl. Rub spice mixture onto both sides of tuna. Place tuna on broiler pan. Broil 4 inches from heat about 10 minutes or until of desired degree of doneness, turning halfway through broiling time. Cover and set aside.

3. For dressing, bring water to a boil in small saucepan over high heat. Add onion; reduce heat to medium-low. Simmer, covered, 4 to 5 minutes or until onion is tender. Add vinegar, mustard, oil and bouillon granules; cook and stir until heated through.

4. Place romaine mixture on 4 salad plates; slice tuna and arrange on top. Drizzle with dressing. Serve warm. *Makes 4 servings*

Seafood Salad Sandwiches

1. In large bowl, combine soup mix, sour cream, celery, mayonnaise, chives, lemon juice, hot pepper sauce and black pepper. Stir in crabmeat; chill.

2. To serve, line rolls with lettuce, then fill with crab mixture.

Makes 4 sandwiches

Variations: Use 1 package (12 ounces) frozen cleaned shrimp, cooked and coarsely chopped; or 2 packages (8 ounces each) sea legs, thawed, drained and chopped; or 1 can (12 ounces) tuna, drained and flaked; or 2 cans (about 4 ounces each) medium or large shrimp, drained and chopped; or 2 cans (6 ounces each) crabmeat, drained and flaked.

1 envelope LIPTON®
  RECIPE SECRETS®
  Vegetable Soup Mix
¾ cup sour cream
½ cup chopped celery
¼ cup HELLMANN'S® or
  BEST FOODS® Real
  Mayonnaise
1 tablespoon fresh
  chopped chives
  (optional)
1 teaspoon lemon juice
  Hot pepper sauce to
  taste
⅛ teaspoon black pepper
2 packages (6 ounces each)
  frozen crabmeat,
  thawed and well
  drained
4 hard rolls, halved
  Lettuce leaves

Galveston Shrimp Salad

2 cups cooked and peeled
medium shrimp

2 large, ripe tomatoes,
peeled and diced

1 cucumber, peeled,
seeded and diced

1 cup diced celery

1 can (4 ounces) chopped
green chiles, drained

$\frac{1}{3}$ cup finely diced onion

2 tablespoons brown sugar

2 tablespoons vegetable oil
Juice of 2 limes

1 jalapeño pepper,* seeded
and finely minced

$\frac{1}{2}$ teaspoon salt

$\frac{1}{2}$ teaspoon celery seed

$\frac{1}{2}$ teaspoon black pepper

2 bay leaves
Dash hot sauce

6 to 8 red leaf lettuce
leaves

*Jalapeño peppers can sting and
irritate the skin, so wear rubber gloves
when handling peppers and do not
touch your eyes.

1. Combine all ingredients except lettuce in large nonreactive bowl; stir well. Cover; refrigerate overnight.

2. Remove and discard bay leaves. Stir salad. Serve on lettuce leaves.

Makes 6 to 8 servings

Serving Suggestion: Serve this salad in martini glasses for a fun presentation.

Salad Niçoise

1 box (9 ounces) BIRDS
EYE® frozen Cut Green
Beans

1 head Boston or green leaf
lettuce

1 can (16 ounces) whole
potatoes, drained and
cut into $\frac{1}{4}$-inch slices

1 can (6$\frac{1}{8}$ ounces) tuna
packed in water,
drained

2 tomatoes, cut into
wedges

$\frac{1}{3}$ cup Greek or black olives

$\frac{1}{3}$ cup Caesar salad dressing

• Cook green beans according to package directions. Drain and rinse under cold water to cool; drain well.

• Arrange lettuce leaves on serving platter. Arrange beans, potatoes, tuna, tomatoes and olives in separate piles on lettuce.

• Drizzle dressing over salad. *Makes about 4 servings*

Prep Time: *5 minutes*
Cook Time: *10 minutes*

Jamaican Seafood Salad

1. Cook noodles according to package directions, omitting salt. Drain and rinse well under cold water until pasta is cool; drain well.

2. Combine crabmeat, shrimp, yellow squash and zucchini in medium bowl.

3. Combine lime peel, juice, vinegar, soy sauce, cilantro, sesame oil, ginger and cinnamon in small bowl; pour over vegetable mixture.

4. Toss to coat evenly. Serve over noodles, chilled or at room temperature.

Makes 6 servings

6 ounces uncooked
   vermicelli noodles
6 ounces fresh or imitation
   crabmeat
4 ounces medium cooked
   shrimp, peeled
1 cup diagonally sliced
   yellow squash
1 cup diagonally sliced
   zucchini
1 teaspoon grated lime
   peel
1 tablespoon lime juice
1 tablespoon rice wine
   vinegar
1 tablespoon soy sauce
1 tablespoon minced fresh
   cilantro
2 teaspoons dark
   sesame oil
2 teaspoons grated fresh
   ginger
$\frac{1}{8}$ teaspoon ground
   cinnamon

Salmon, Asparagus & Orzo Salad

1. Prepare grill for direct grilling. Grill salmon on oiled grid over medium coals about 10 minutes per inch of thickness or until opaque. Remove from grill; cool. Flake salmon into bite-size pieces.

2. Meanwhile, cook orzo according to package directions; cool.

3. Combine salmon, orzo, asparagus, cranberries and green onions in large bowl. Whisk together olive oil, vinegar, mustard, salt and pepper in small bowl until well blended. Pour over salmon mixture; toss until coated. Chill 30 minutes to 1 hour. Serve over lettuce, if desired.

Makes 4 to 6 servings

1 (8-ounce) salmon fillet
1 cup uncooked orzo pasta
8 ounces asparagus spears,
   cut into 2-inch lengths
   (about 1$\frac{1}{2}$ cups),
   cooked
$\frac{1}{2}$ cup dried cranberries
$\frac{1}{4}$ cup sliced green onions
3 tablespoons olive oil
1 tablespoon white wine
   vinegar
1$\frac{1}{2}$ teaspoons Dijon mustard
$\frac{1}{2}$ teaspoon salt
$\frac{1}{8}$ teaspoon black pepper

California Crab Salad

1 packet (0.4 ounce)
  HIDDEN VALLEY® The
  Original Ranch®
  Buttermilk Recipe
  Salad Dressing Mix
1 cup buttermilk
1 cup mayonnaise
1 tablespoon grated fresh
  ginger
1 teaspoon prepared
  horseradish
2 cups cooked white rice,
  chilled
4 lettuce leaves
8 ounces cooked crabmeat,
  chilled
1 large ripe avocado, thinly
  sliced
½ medium cucumber, thinly
  sliced

In medium bowl, whisk together salad dressing mix, buttermilk and mayonnaise. Whisk in ginger and horseradish. Cover and refrigerate 30 minutes. To serve, arrange ½ cup rice on top of each lettuce leaf. Top with 2 tablespoons of the dressing. Arrange one-quarter of the crabmeat, avocado and cucumber on top of each rice mound. Serve with remaining dressing. Garnish with cherry tomatoes, if desired. *Makes 4 servings*

Sandwiches & Salads

Tuna Schooners

1. Combine tuna, apple and carrot in medium bowl. Add salad dressing; stir to combine.

2. Spread ¼ of tuna mixture over top of each muffin half. Stand 2 crackers and press firmly into tuna mixture on each muffin half to form "sails."

Makes 4 servings

1 can (6 ounces) tuna packed in water, drained and flaked
½ cup finely chopped apple
¼ cup shredded carrot
⅓ cup ranch salad dressing
2 English muffins, split and lightly toasted
8 triangular-shaped baked whole wheat crackers or triangular-shaped tortilla chips

Spinach, Shrimp and Cantaloupe Salad

¾ pound cooked peeled
shrimp, cut into
bite-size pieces
4 cups (about 6 ounces)
baby spinach leaves
1 cup ½-inch-diced
cantaloupe cubes
(about ⅓ of medium
cantaloupe)
¼ cup orange juice
1 small shallot, minced
1½ tablespoons canola oil
1 tablespoon balsamic
vinegar
1 teaspoon powdered sugar
1 teaspoon poppy seeds
⅛ teaspoon salt
⅛ teaspoon black pepper
⅛ teaspoon red pepper
flakes (optional)

1. Combine shrimp, spinach and cantaloupe in large salad bowl.

2. Combine orange juice, shallot, oil, vinegar, sugar, poppy seeds, salt, pepper and red pepper flakes, if desired, in small bowl. Stir well. Pour over salad just before serving. Toss gently, but thoroughly. *Makes 4 servings*

Southwestern Tuna Salad "Subs"

1. Flake tuna with fork in medium bowl. Stir in bell peppers, cheese, mayonnaise, bacon bits, olives and cilantro.

2. To serve, divide evenly among lettuce leaves. Fold each lettuce leaf lengthwise for hand-held tuna "sub sandwich."

Makes 4 servings

1 can (6 ounces) tuna packed in water, drained
½ cup finely chopped red bell pepper
½ cup finely chopped green bell pepper
⅓ cup shredded sharp Cheddar cheese
3 tablespoons mayonnaise
2 tablespoons bacon bits
1 tablespoon plus 1 teaspoon chopped black olives
1 tablespoon chopped fresh cilantro
4 long (9- to-10-inch) romaine lettuce leaves

Grilled Salmon Salad with Orange-Basil Vinaigrette

¼ cup frozen orange juice concentrate, thawed

1 tablespoon plus
1½ teaspoons white wine vinegar or cider vinegar

1 tablespoon chopped fresh basil *or*
1 teaspoon dried basil

1½ teaspoons olive oil

1 salmon fillet (about 8 ounces)

4 cups torn mixed greens

¾ cup sliced strawberries

10 to 12 thin cucumber slices, cut into halves

⅛ teaspoon coarsely ground black pepper

1. Whisk together juice concentrate, vinegar, basil and olive oil. Set aside 2 tablespoons juice concentrate mixture. Reserve remaining mixture to use as salad dressing.

2. Prepare grill for direct grilling. Grill salmon, skin side down, on oiled grid over medium coals 5 minutes. Turn and grill 5 minutes or until fish begins to flake, brushing frequently with 2 tablespoons juice concentrate mixture. Cool slightly.

3. Toss together greens, strawberries and cucumber in large bowl. Divide mixture between two serving plates.

4. Remove skin from salmon. Break salmon into chunks; arrange on greens mixture. Drizzle with reserved juice concentrate mixture. Sprinkle with pepper.

Makes 2 servings

Scallop and Yellow Rice Salad

1. Combine jalapeño peppers and garlic in food processor or blender. Process until finely minced.

2. Heat 2 tablespoons oil in large saucepan over medium heat. Add onion and jalapeño pepper mixture. Cook and stir 3 to 4 minutes or until onion is softened. Add water, salt, turmeric and cumin. Bring mixture to a boil over high heat; add rice. Cover; reduce heat to low. Simmer 15 to 20 minutes or until most of the liquid is absorbed.

3. Stir in scallops; cover. Simmer 2 to 3 minutes or until scallops turn opaque and are cooked through.

4. Transfer rice mixture to large bowl; set bowl in ice water to chill rice and prevent scallops from overcooking.

5. Toss mixture every few minutes. When mixture is lukewarm, stir in beans, tomatoes and cilantro.

6. Combine remaining ⅓ cup oil and lime juice in 1-cup glass measure. Pour over salad and toss. Serve immediately or refrigerate and serve chilled. Garnish with lime wedges just before serving.   *Makes 5 servings*

2 jalapeño or serrano peppers,* seeded
1 clove garlic, peeled
⅓ cup plus 2 tablespoons vegetable oil, divided
½ cup chopped onion
2 cups water
½ teaspoon salt
½ teaspoon ground turmeric
½ teaspoon ground cumin
1 cup uncooked long-grain white rice
1 pound bay scallops or quartered sea scallops
1 can (about 15 ounces) black beans, rinsed and drained
1 cup chopped tomatoes
¼ cup chopped fresh cilantro or parsley
3 tablespoons lime juice
Lime wedges

Jalapeño and other chili peppers can sting and irritate the skin, so wear rubber gloves when handling peppers and do not touch your eyes.

Tuna Melts

1. Preheat broiler. Combine tuna, coleslaw mix and green onions in medium bowl. Combine mayonnaise, mustard and dill weed in small bowl. Stir mayonnaise mixture into tuna mixture. Spread tuna mixture onto muffin halves. Place on broiler pan.

2. Broil 4 inches from heat 3 to 4 minutes or until heated through. Sprinkle with cheese. Broil 1 to 2 minutes more or until cheese melts.   *Makes 4 servings*

1 can (12 ounces) chunk white tuna packed in water, drained and flaked
1½ cups packaged coleslaw mix
3 tablespoons sliced green onions
3 tablespoons mayonnaise
1 tablespoon Dijon mustard
1 teaspoon dried dill weed
4 English muffins, split and lightly toasted
⅓ cup shredded Cheddar cheese

Main-Dish Mediterranean Salad

1 package (10 ounces)
  romaine lettuce
1 can (6 ounces) solid
  white tuna packed in
  water, drained and
  flaked
½ pound fresh green beans,
  cooked and drained,
  or 1 can (14½ ounces)
  whole green beans,
  drained
1 carton (8 ounces) cherry
  tomatoes, halved

Dressing

2 tablespoons olive oil
2 tablespoons rice or apple
  cider vinegar
1½ teaspoons Dijon mustard
½ teaspoon black pepper

1. Place lettuce, tuna, green beans and tomatoes in large salad bowl.

2. Whisk oil, vinegar, mustard and pepper in a small bowl to blend.

3. Pour dressing over salad, and toss well.

4. Mound 3 cups of salad on 4 large plates to serve.   *Makes 4 servings*

Serving Suggestion: Make this into a complete meal by serving with fresh focaccia rolls or a crusty French bread.

Hot Crab and Cheese on Muffins

1. Preheat broiler. Place muffin halves on lightly greased baking sheet. Broil 4 inches from heat 2 minutes or until muffins are lightly toasted. Place on large microwavable plate.

2. Melt butter in medium skillet over medium heat. Add green onions and bell pepper; cook and stir 3 to 4 minutes or until tender. Remove from heat; stir in crabmeat, hot pepper sauce and cheeses. Spoon about ⅓ cup crab mixture onto muffin halves.

3. Microwave on HIGH 2 to 3 minutes, rotating platter once, or until crab mixture is heated through.   *Makes 8 servings*

Prep and Cook Time: *12 minutes*

**4 English muffins, split
1 tablespoon butter or
   margarine
3 green onions, chopped
⅓ cup chopped red bell
   pepper
½ pound fresh crabmeat,
   drained and flaked***
**1 to 2 teaspoons hot
   pepper sauce
1 cup (4 ounces) shredded
   Cheddar cheese
1 cup (4 ounces) shredded
   Monterey Jack cheese**

*Two cans (6 ounces each) fancy crabmeat, drained, can be substituted for fresh crabmeat.

Tuna, Fennel and Pasta Salad

¾ pound yellow fin tuna
    steaks
2 teaspoons Dijon mustard
8 ounces small pasta shells,
    cooked and cooled
4 cups torn red leaf lettuce
2 cups cut asparagus
    spears, cooked crisp-
    tender and cooled
½ cup thinly sliced fennel
    bulb
½ cup thinly sliced red bell
    pepper
8 cherry tomatoes, halved
    Prepared balsamic
    vinaigrette
    Salt and black pepper

1. Brush sides of tuna with mustard. Grill tuna over medium-hot coals, or broil 6 inches from heat source about 5 minutes on each side or until fish begins to flake when tested with fork. Break into chunks.

2. Toss tuna, pasta, lettuce, asparagus, fennel, bell pepper and tomatoes in large bowl; drizzle with balsamic vinaigrette and toss. Season to taste with salt and black pepper.

Makes 4 main-dish servings

Fresh Rockfish Burgers

1. Finely chop rockfish and place in medium bowl. Add egg white, bread crumbs, green onion, parsley, lime juice, capers, mustard, salt and pepper; gently combine with fork. Shape into 4 patties.

2. Spray heavy grillproof cast iron skillet or griddle with nonstick cooking spray; place on grid over hot coals to heat. Spray tops of burgers with additional cooking spray. Place burgers in hot skillet; grill on covered grill over hot coals 4 to 5 minutes or until burgers are browned on both sides, turning once. Serve on English muffins with lettuce, tomato slices and Dijon mustard, if desired.

Makes 4 servings

½ **pound skinless rockfish or scrod fillet**
1 **egg white**
¼ **cup plain dry bread crumbs**
1 **green onion, finely chopped**
1 **tablespoon finely chopped fresh parsley**
2 **teaspoons fresh lime juice**
1½ **teaspoons capers**
1 **teaspoon Dijon mustard**
¼ **teaspoon salt**
⅛ **teaspoon black pepper Nonstick cooking spray**
4 **grilled whole wheat English muffins**
4 **leaves green leaf lettuce**
8 **tomato slices Additional Dijon mustard for serving (optional)**

Sandwiches & Salads

Weeknight Meals

Shrimp Scampi

⅓ cup clarified butter*
4 tablespoons minced garlic
1½ pounds large raw shrimp, peeled and deveined
6 green onions, thinly sliced
¼ cup dry white wine
2 tablespoons lemon juice
8 large sprigs fresh parsley, finely chopped
Salt and black pepper
Lemon slices and fresh parsley sprigs (optional)

*To clarify butter, melt butter over low heat. Skim off the white foam that forms on top, then strain clear golden butter through cheesecloth into container. Discard milky residue at the bottom of pan. Clarified butter will keep, covered, in refrigerator for up to 2 months.

1. Heat clarified butter in large skillet over medium heat. Add garlic; cook and stir 1 to 2 minutes or until soft but not brown. Add shrimp, green onions, wine and lemon juice; cook 2 to 4 minutes or until shrimp turn pink and opaque, stirring occasionally. Do not overcook.

2. Add chopped parsley; season with salt and pepper. Garnish with lemon slices and parsley sprigs, if desired.

Makes 4 servings

2 cans (12 ounces each) tuna packed in water, drained and flaked
3 cups diced celery
3 cups crushed potato chips, divided
6 hard-cooked eggs, chopped
1 can (10¾ ounces) condensed cream of mushroom soup, undiluted
1 can (10¾ ounces) condensed cream of celery soup, undiluted
1 cup mayonnaise
1 teaspoon dried tarragon leaves
1 teaspoon black pepper

Weeknight Meals

Mom's Tuna Casserole

Slow Cooker Directions

1. Combine tuna, celery, 2½ cups potato chips, eggs, soups, mayonnaise, tarragon and pepper in slow cooker; stir well.

2. Cover; cook on LOW 5 to 8 hours.

3. Sprinkle with remaining ½ cup potato chips. _Makes 8 servings_

Thyme-Roasted Salmon with Horseradish-Dijon Sour Cream

1. Preheat oven to 400°F.

2. Line a baking sheet with foil. Arrange fillets on foil, then sprinkle evenly with oil, thyme and lemon pepper seasoning salt. Bake 12 to 14 minutes or until center is opaque.

3. Meanwhile, combine remaining ingredients in a small bowl; stir to blend well. Serve sauce alongside fillets.

Makes 2 servings

2 (6-ounce) salmon fillets, rinsed and patted dry
1 tablespoon extra-virgin olive oil
½ teaspoon dried thyme
½ teaspoon lemon pepper
⅓ cup sour cream
2 tablespoons mayonnaise
2 teaspoons prepared horseradish
½ teaspoon Worcestershire sauce
½ teaspoon Dijon mustard
¼ teaspoon salt

Weeknight Meals

Bacon-Wrapped Scallops on Angel Hair Pasta

1 bacon slice, cut
    crosswise into thirds
3 sea scallops (2 ounces)
2 ounces uncooked angel
    hair pasta
1 tablespoon butter
2 green onions with tops,
    sliced
1 clove garlic, minced
    Black pepper or garlic
    pepper, to taste

1. Wrap one bacon piece around each scallop; secure with toothpick.

2. Cook pasta according to package directions. Drain pasta; return to pan.

3. Meanwhile, heat small nonstick skillet over medium heat. Add scallops; cook 2 to 3 minutes on each side or until bacon is crisp and scallops are opaque. Remove scallops from skillet; discard toothpicks. Reduce heat to low.

4. Melt butter in same skillet. Add green onions and garlic; cook and stir 1 minute or until green onion is tender. Remove from heat.

5. Add onion mixture to pasta; toss lightly. Place on serving plate. Top with scallops. Season with pepper. *Makes 1 serving*

Pecan Catfish with Cranberry Sauce

1. Preheat oven to 425°F. Place pecans and flour in bowl of food processor; pulse just until finely chopped. *Do not overprocess.* Place pecan mixture in shallow dish or plate. Whisk eggs and water in another shallow dish. Sprinkle salt and pepper on both sides of each fillet; dip first in egg, then in pecan mixture, pressing to make coating stick.

2. Place 1 tablespoon butter in 13×9-inch pan or baking dish large enough to hold fillets in single layer. Melt butter in oven and tilt pan to distribute evenly.

3. Place fillets in prepared pan. Dot with remaining 1 tablespoon butter. Bake 15 to 20 minutes or until fish begins to flake when tested with fork. Serve with cranberry sauce.   *Makes 4 servings*

1½ cup pecans
2 tablespoons flour
1 egg
2 tablespoons water
  Salt and pepper
4 catfish fillets (about
  1¼ pounds)
2 tablespoons butter,
  divided
  Prepared cranberry sauce

Thai Seafood Stir-Fry

2 tablespoons lemon juice
1 tablespoon cornstarch
1 tablespoon soy sauce
2 teaspoons sugar
½ teaspoon ground ginger
¼ teaspoon red pepper
    flakes
8 ounces broccoli
2 stalks celery
1 large onion
3 tablespoons vegetable oil
¼ cup water
1 pound surimi seafood
    chunks or imitation
    crabmeat, thawed if
    frozen
½ cup sliced water
    chestnuts
3 cups hot cooked rice

1. Combine lemon juice, cornstarch, soy sauce, sugar, ginger and red pepper flakes in small bowl; stir until smooth. Set aside.

2. Remove woody stems from broccoli; discard. Cut tops into small florets; rinse. Cut celery diagonally into ½-inch slices. Cut onion lengthwise in half; cut crosswise into slices.

3. Heat wok over high heat about 1 minute or until hot. Drizzle oil into wok and heat 30 seconds. Add onion; stir-fry 1 minute. Add broccoli and celery; stir-fry 2 minutes. Reduce heat to medium-high. Add water; cover and cook until vegetables are crisp-tender. Add surimi and water chestnuts; stir-fry gently 1 minute to combine.

4. Stir lemon juice mixture until smooth and add to wok. Stir-fry until sauce boils and thickens. Spoon into serving dish or place wok on table over wok ring stand or trivet. Serve with rice. *Makes 6 servings*

Note: Surimi seafood is processed fish, typically pollack, that is flavored and restructured to make seafood products. It comes in flakes, chunks, sticks or nuggets. This convenient seafood product is wonderful for creating quick, delicious meals such as this one.

Shrimp and Pepper Noodle Bowl

1. Place 4 cups water in large saucepan; bring to a boil over high heat. Remove seasoning packets from noodles; set aside. Break up ramen noodles; add to water. Add shrimp and bell pepper; cook 3 minutes.

2. Add seasoning packets, green onions, soy sauce and hot pepper sauce. Cook 1 minute. Garnish with cilantro, if desired.   *Makes 4 servings*

2 packages (3 ounces each) shrimp-flavored instant ramen noodle soup mix
8 ounces frozen medium cooked shrimp *or* 1 package (8 ounces) frozen cooked baby shrimp
1 cup frozen bell pepper strips, cut into bite-size pieces
¼ cup chopped green onions
1 tablespoon soy sauce
½ teaspoon hot pepper sauce
2 tablespoons chopped cilantro (optional)

Quick Pasta Puttanesca

1 package (16 ounces) uncooked spaghetti

3 tablespoons plus 1 teaspoon olive oil, divided

¼ to 1 teaspoon red pepper flakes*

2 cans (6 ounces each) chunk light tuna packed in water, drained

1 tablespoon dried minced onion

1 teaspoon minced garlic

1 can (28 ounces) diced tomatoes

1 can (8 ounces) tomato sauce

24 pitted kalamata or black olives

2 tablespoons capers, drained

*For a mildly spicy dish, use ¼ teaspoon red pepper. For a very spicy dish, use 1 teaspoon red pepper.

1. Cook spaghetti according to package directions; drain. Return spaghetti to saucepan; add 1 teaspoon oil and toss to coat.

2. Meanwhile, heat remaining 3 tablespoons oil in large skillet over medium-high heat. Add red pepper flakes; cook and stir 1 to 2 minutes or until sizzling. Add tuna; cook and stir 2 to 3 minutes. Add onion and garlic; cook and stir 1 minute. Add tomatoes with juice, tomato sauce, olives and capers. Cook over medium-high heat, stirring frequently, until sauce is heated through.

3. Add sauce to pasta; mix well.

Makes 6 to 8 servings

Salmon-Potato Cakes with Mustard Tartar Sauce

1. Halve potatoes (leave skin on) and place in small saucepan with about ½ cup water. Bring to a boil, reduce heat and simmer until potatoes are tender, about 15 minutes. Drain any remaining water. Mash potatoes with fork, leaving chunky texture.

2. Combine mashed potatoes, salmon, egg white, green onions, parsley and seasoning mix in medium mixing bowl.

3. Heat oil in nonstick skillet over medium heat. Fill half-cup measuring cup with mixture. Turn mixture out into skillet and flatten slightly with spatula. Repeat for second cake. Cook until browned and flip to brown other side, about 7 minutes total.

4. Meanwhile, combine all ingredients for sauce in small bowl; mix well. Serve cakes with sauce.

Makes 2 servings

3 small red potatoes (8 ounces)
1 cup cooked flaked salmon
1 egg white
2 green onions, chopped
1 tablespoon chopped fresh parsley
½ teaspoon Cajun or Creole seasoning mix
1 teaspoon olive or canola oil

Mustard Tartar Sauce

1 tablespoon mayonnaise
1 tablespoon plain yogurt or sour cream
1 tablespoon chopped fresh parsley
1 tablespoon chopped dill pickle
2 teaspoons coarse-grain mustard
1 teaspoon lemon juice

Stewed Catfish and Bell Peppers

1½ pounds catfish fillets or other firm white-fleshed fish
1 onion, chopped
1 *each* green and red bell pepper, cut into 1-inch pieces
1 clove garlic, minced
1 cup clam juice
1 tomato, chopped
¼ cup *Frank's® RedHot®* Original Cayenne Pepper Sauce
2 tablespoons minced parsley

1. On sheet of waxed paper, mix *2 tablespoons flour* with ½ *teaspoon salt.* Lightly coat fillets with flour mixture; set aside.

2. Heat *1 tablespoon oil* in large nonstick skillet until hot. Add onion, peppers and garlic. Cook and stir 3 minutes or until crisp-tender; transfer to dish.

3. Heat *1 tablespoon oil* in same skillet until hot. Cook fillets 5 minutes or until golden brown, turning once. Return vegetables to skillet. Add clam juice, tomato, *Frank's RedHot* Sauce and parsley. Heat to boiling. Reduce heat to medium-low. Cook, covered, 8 to 10 minutes or until fish flakes with fork. Serve with hot cooked rice, if desired. *Makes 6 servings*

Prep Time: *15 minutes*
Cook Time: *20 minutes*

Swordfish Pomodoro

1. Season fish with salt and pepper. Dust fish in flour; set aside.

2. Heat olive oil in large skillet over medium heat. Add onions; cook and stir 4 minutes or until tender. Add garlic; cook and stir 30 seconds. Add tomatoes; cook 3 minutes, stirring occasionally. Stir in giardiniera, wine, if desired, oregano and ¼ teaspoon salt. Cook about 3 minutes or until most of liquid has evaporated.

3. Meanwhile, heat canola oil in 12-inch nonstick skillet over medium-high heat. Cook fish 4 minutes; turn and cook 3 to 4 minutes more or until fish just begins to flake when tested with fork. Serve tomato mixture over fish.

Makes 6 servings

Prep Time: *10 minutes*
Cook Time: *20 minutes*

1½ pounds swordfish steaks
 (¾ inch thick)
 Salt and black pepper
1 tablespoon all-purpose
 flour
2 teaspoons olive oil
1 medium onion, halved
 and cut into thin slices
1 clove garlic, minced
1½ cups chopped seeded
 tomatoes
⅓ cup drained mild
 giardiniera*
2 tablespoons dry white
 wine (optional)
1 tablespoon chopped
 fresh oregano *or*
 1 teaspoon dried
 oregano
2 tablespoons canola oil

Giardiniera is Italian pickled vegetables. Available mild or hot, giardiniera is in the pickle or ethnic foods section of the grocery store.

Spicy Crabmeat Frittata

1. Preheat broiler. Heat oil in 10-inch nonstick skillet with ovenproof handle over medium-high heat. Add bell pepper and garlic; cook and stir 3 minutes or until soft.

2. Meanwhile, beat eggs in medium bowl. Break up large pieces of crabmeat. Add crabmeat, black pepper, salt and hot pepper sauce to eggs; blend well. Set aside.

3. Add tomato to skillet; cook and stir 1 minute. Add egg mixture. Reduce heat to medium-low; cook about 7 minutes or until eggs begin to set around edges.

4. Remove pan from burner and place under broiler 6 inches from heat. Broil about 2 minutes or until frittata is set and top is browned. Remove from broiler; slide frittata onto serving plate. Serve immediately.

Makes 4 servings

Serving Suggestion: Serve with crusty bread, cut-up raw vegetables and guacamole.

Prep & Cook Time: *20 minutes*

1 tablespoon olive oil
1 medium green bell
 pepper, finely chopped
2 cloves garlic, minced
6 eggs
1 can (6½ ounces) lump
 white crabmeat,
 drained
¼ teaspoon black pepper
¼ teaspoon salt
¼ teaspoon hot pepper
 sauce
1 large ripe plum tomato,
 seeded and finely
 chopped

Santa Fe Fish Fillets with Mango-Cilantro Salsa

Nonstick cooking spray
1½ pounds fish fillets (cod, perch or tilapia, about ½ inch thick)
½ package (3 tablespoons) ORTEGA® Taco Seasoning Mix
3 ORTEGA® Taco Shells, finely crushed
1 cup ORTEGA® Salsa, any variety
½ cup diced mango
2 tablespoons chopped cilantro

PREHEAT oven to 375°F. Cover broiler pan with foil. Spray with cooking spray.

DIP fish fillets in taco seasoning mix, coating both sides; place on foil. Spray coated fillets with cooking spray. Sprinkle with crushed taco shells.

BAKE 15 to 20 minutes until flaky in center.

MICROWAVE salsa on HIGH (100%) 1 minute. Stir in mango and cilantro.

SPOON salsa over fish when serving.   *Makes 6 servings*

Note: Refrigerated jars of sliced mango can be found in the produce section at most supermarkets.

Sweet and Sour Shrimp Stir-Fry

1. Heat oil in large nonstick skillet over medium heat. Add celery, bell pepper, green onions and ginger. Cook and stir 5 to 7 minutes.

2. Add lemon juice, soy sauce and sugar; cook and stir 1 minute. Add shrimp; cook 3 minutes or until shrimp are pink and opaque.   *Makes 4 servings*

1 tablespoon sesame oil
½ cup chopped celery
¼ cup chopped red bell pepper
¼ cup chopped green onions
½ teaspoon ground ginger
1 teaspoon lemon juice
1 teaspoon soy sauce
¼ teaspoon sugar
1 pound medium raw shrimp, peeled and deveined, tails intact

Tuna and Broccoli Bake

Place broccoli on bottom of 2-quart baking dish. Top with bread cubes and tuna. In medium bowl, combine cottage cheese, Cheddar cheese, eggs and pepper. Spread evenly over tuna mixture. Bake in 400°F oven 30 minutes or until golden brown and puffed.

Makes 4 servings

Prep Time: *35 minutes*

1 package (16 ounces) frozen broccoli cuts, thawed and well drained

2 slices bread, cut in ½-inch cubes

1 (7-ounce) STARKIST Flavor Fresh Pouch® Tuna (Albacore or Chunk Light)

2 cups cottage cheese

1 cup shredded Cheddar cheese

3 eggs

¼ teaspoon ground black pepper

Weeknight Meals

Lemon Salmon and Spinach Pasta

1. Pat salmon dry with paper towels. Remove skin from salmon; discard. Cut fish into ½-inch pieces.

2. Cook fettuccine according to package directions, omitting salt. Drain and return to hot saucepan.

3. Meanwhile, melt butter in large skillet over medium-high heat. Add salmon, lemon peel, red pepper flakes and garlic; cook 4 to 7 minutes or until salmon begins to flake when tested with fork. Gently stir in lemon juice.

4. Add salmon mixture, spinach and carrot to hot cooked fettuccine; gently toss to combine. Serve immediately. *Makes 4 servings*

Prep Time: *15 minutes*
Cook Time: *4 to 7 minutes*

¾ **pound salmon fillet**
8 **ounces uncooked fettuccine**
4 **teaspoons butter**
1 **teaspoon finely grated lemon peel**
¼ **teaspoon red pepper flakes**
2 **cloves garlic, minced**
2 **tablespoons lemon juice**
3 **cups baby spinach leaves**
½ **cup shredded carrot**

Steamed Fish Fillets with Black Bean Sauce

1½ pounds white-fleshed fish fillets (Lake Superior whitefish, halibut, rainbow trout or catfish)
1 tablespoon vegetable oil
2 green onions, chopped
2 tablespoons chopped fresh ginger
2 tablespoons black bean sauce (see note)
Green onion tops (optional)

1. Fill large saucepan about one-third full with water. Place bamboo steamer basket over saucepan. Or, fill wok fitted with rack about one-third full with water. Cover and bring water to a boil. Place fillets in single layer on platter that fits into steamer or wok.

2. Heat oil in small skillet until hot. Add green onions, ginger and black bean sauce; cook, stirring about 30 seconds or just until fragrant. Immediately pour contents of skillet evenly over fillets. Place platter in steamer; cover and steam 10 to 15 minutes or until fish is opaque in center.

3. Serve fillets and sauce over rice, if desired. Garnish with green onion tops, if desired.

Makes 4 servings

Note: Jarred black bean sauce is sold in the Asian food section of most large supermarkets. It is made of fermented black soybeans, soy sauce, garlic, sherry, sesame oil and ginger. Black soybeans have a pungent odor and a unique, pronounced flavor. Do not substitute regular black beans.

Trout with Apples and Toasted Hazelnuts

1. Preheat oven to 375°F. Place hazelnuts on baking sheet; bake 8 minutes or until lightly browned. Quickly transfer nuts to clean dry dish towel. Fold towel over nuts; rub vigorously to remove as much of skins as possible. Using food processor, finely chop hazelnuts.

2. Melt 3 tablespoons butter in medium skillet over medium-high heat. Add apple; cook 4 to 5 minutes or until crisp-tender. Remove from skillet with slotted spoon; set aside.

3. Rinse trout and pat dry with paper towels. Sprinkle fish with salt and pepper, then coat in flour. Place fish in skillet. Cook 4 minutes or until golden and fish flakes easily when tested with fork, turning halfway through cooking time. Return apple to skillet. Reduce heat to low and keep warm.

4. Melt remaining 2 tablespoons butter in small saucepan over low heat. Stir in lemon juice, chives and hazelnuts. To serve, sprinkle fish and apple with hazelnut mixture. Garnish as desired. *Makes 2 servings*

⅓ cup whole hazelnuts
5 tablespoons butter or margarine, divided
1 large Red Delicious apple, cored and cut into 16 wedges
2 butterflied rainbow trout fillets (about 8 ounces each)
Salt and black pepper
3 tablespoons all-purpose flour
1 tablespoon lemon juice
1 tablespoon snipped fresh chives
Lemon slices and fresh chives (optional)

Crab-Artichoke Casserole

8 ounces uncooked small shell pasta
2 tablespoons butter
6 green onions, chopped
2 tablespoons all-purpose flour
1 cup half-and-half
1 teaspoon dry mustard
½ teaspoon ground red pepper
Salt and black pepper
½ cup (2 ounces) shredded Swiss cheese, divided
1 package (about 8 ounces) imitation crabmeat
1 can (about 14 ounces) artichoke hearts, drained and cut into bite-size pieces

1. Preheat oven to 350°F. Grease 2-quart casserole. Cook pasta according to package directions; drain and set aside.

2. Melt butter in large saucepan over medium heat. Add green onions; cook and stir about 2 minutes. Add flour; cook and stir 2 minutes more. Gradually add half-and-half, whisking constantly until mixture begins to thicken. Whisk in mustard and ground red pepper; season to taste with salt and black pepper. Remove from heat; stir in ¼ cup cheese until melted.

3. Combine crabmeat, artichokes and pasta in prepared casserole. Add sauce mixture; stir until blended. Top with remaining ¼ cup cheese. Bake about 40 minutes or until hot, bubbly and lightly browned. *Makes 6 servings*

Serving Suggestion: This can also be baked in individual ovenproof dishes. Reduce cooking time to about 20 minutes.

Curried Shrimp and Noodles

1. Bring water to boil in large saucepan. Add soup mix, shrimp, bell pepper, green onions, salt and black pepper.

2. Cook 3 to 5 minutes, stirring frequently, or until noodles are tender. Stir in lime juice. Serve immediately.

Makes 4 servings

3 cups water
2 packages (about 1.6 ounces each) instant curry-flavored rice noodle soup mix
1 package (8 ounces) frozen cooked baby shrimp
1 cup frozen bell pepper strips, cut into 1-inch pieces or 1 cup frozen peas
¼ cup chopped green onions
¼ teaspoon salt
¼ teaspoon black pepper
1 to 2 tablespoons fresh lime juice

Lickety-Split Paella Pronto

1 tablespoon olive oil
1 large onion, chopped
2 cloves garlic, minced
1 jar (16 ounces) salsa
1 can (about 14 ounces) diced tomatoes
1 can (14 ounces) artichoke hearts, drained and quartered
1 can (14 ounces) chicken broth
1 package (about 8 ounces) uncooked yellow rice
1 can (12 ounces) solid white tuna packed in water, drained and flaked
1 package (9 to 10 ounces) frozen green peas

1. Heat oil in large nonstick skillet over medium heat. Add onion and garlic; cook and stir about 5 minutes or until onion is tender.

2. Stir in salsa, tomatoes with juice, artichokes, broth and rice. Bring to a boil. Cover; reduce heat to low and simmer 15 minutes.

3. Stir in tuna and peas. Cover; cook 5 to 10 minutes or until rice is tender and tuna and peas are heated through. Garnish as desired.

Makes 4 to 6 servings

Speedy Salmon Patties

1. Drain salmon well, reserving 2 tablespoons liquid. Place salmon in medium bowl; break apart with fork. Add reserved liquid, green onions, egg, dill and garlic; mix well.

2. Combine flour and baking powder in small bowl; add to salmon mixture. Stir until well blended. Shape mixture into 6 patties.

3. Heat oil in large skillet to 350°F. Add salmon patties; cook until golden brown on both sides. Remove from oil; drain on paper towels. Serve warm.

Makes 6 patties

1 can (12 ounces) pink
   salmon, undrained
¼ cup minced green onions
1 egg, lightly beaten
1 tablespoon chopped
   fresh dill
1 clove garlic, minced
½ cup all-purpose flour
1½ teaspoons baking powder
1½ cups vegetable oil

Lemon Catfish Bake

3 tablespoons I CAN'T BELIEVE IT'S NOT BUTTER!® Spread, melted
1 teaspoon LAWRY'S® Lemon Pepper
½ teaspoon LAWRY'S® Seasoned Salt
¼ teaspoon dried dill weed
1 pound catfish or tilapia fillets
½ cup plain dry bread crumbs
Paprika (optional)

Preheat oven to 350°. In shallow dish, combine Spread, Lemon Pepper, Seasoned Salt and dill weed. Dip fillets in Spread mixture, then evenly coat with bread crumbs.

In 13×9-inch baking dish sprayed with nonstick cooking spray, arrange fillets. Lightly sprinkle, if desired, with paprika. Bake 30 minutes or until fish flakes with a fork. Garnish, if desired, with lemon slices. *Makes 4 servings*

Prep. Time: *10 minutes*
Cook Time: *25 to 30 minutes*

Stir-Fried Crab Legs

1. Soak crab legs in water for 30 minutes to leach out salt brine used for packaging. Cut crab legs into 2-inch-long pieces with poultry scissors or cleaver.

2. Combine water, sherry, soy sauce, cornstarch and sugar in small bowl. Set aside.

3. Heat wok over high heat about 1 minute. Drizzle oil into wok; heat 15 seconds. Add ginger; stir-fry about 1 minute to flavor oil. Remove and discard ginger. Add crab pieces and garlic. Stir-fry 5 minutes.

4. Stir cornstarch mixture and pour into wok. Add green onions and toss. Cook and stir until sauce boils and thickens. Transfer to serving platter. Serve with lemon wedges. *Makes 3 to 4 servings*

Note: To extract meat from legs, snip along each side of shell with scissors and lift out meat with skewer before serving. Reheat meat in wok for a few seconds. Or, to save time, serve in the shell with seafood shell crackers. Have guests crack the shells and remove meat with small seafood forks.

1½ pounds frozen Alaskan king crab legs, thawed and drained
½ cup water
2 tablespoons dry sherry
2 tablespoons soy sauce
1 tablespoon cornstarch
1 teaspoon sugar
3 tablespoons vegetable oil
1 piece fresh ginger (about 1-inch square), peeled and cut into 4 slices
2 cloves garlic, minced
3 green onion tops, cut into 1-inch lengths
Lemon wedges

2 cups cooked rice
2 cans (6 ounces each)
    tuna packed in water,
    drained and flaked
1 cup mayonnaise
1 cup (4 ounces) shredded
    Cheddar cheese
1 can (4 ounces) sliced
    black olives
½ cup thinly sliced celery
½ cup sour cream
2 tablespoons dried onion
1 refrigerated pie crust
    dough

Cheesy Tuna Pie

1. Preheat oven to 350°F. Spray 9-inch deep-dish pie pan with nonstick cooking spray.

2. Combine all ingredients except pie dough in medium bowl; mix well. Spoon into prepared pan. Place pie dough over tuna mixture; press edge to pan to seal. Cut slits for steam to escape.

3. Bake 20 minutes or until crust is browned and filling is bubbly.

Makes 6 servings

Note: This is recipe is super easy! It uses pantry staple ingredients and has a wonderful made-from-scratch flavor.

Shrimp Bowls

1. Combine rice, water and salt in small saucepan with tight-fitting lid. Bring to a boil. Reduce heat to low; cover and cook 15 minutes or until rice is tender and liquid is absorbed. Keep warm.

2. Heat vegetable oil in large skillet over medium-high heat. Add vegetables; stir-fry 3 minutes or until crisp-tender. Stir in shrimp. Combine sweet and sour sauce and soy sauce in small bowl. Pour over shrimp mixture; heat through.

3. To serve, mound rice onto 4 plates and press down in center to form "bowls." Spoon shrimp mixture into "bowls."   *Makes 4 servings*

¾ cup short-grain rice
1 cup plus 2 tablespoons water
¼ teaspoon salt
1 tablespoon vegetable oil
2 cups frozen stir-fry vegetables
1 (12-ounce) package cooked baby shrimp, thawed if frozen and drained
⅓ to ½ cup prepared sweet and sour sauce, to taste
1 tablespoon soy sauce

Hazelnut-Coated Salmon Steaks

¼ cup hazelnuts
4 salmon steaks (about
   5 ounces each)
1 tablespoon apple butter
1 tablespoon Dijon
   mustard
¼ teaspoon dried thyme
⅛ teaspoon black pepper

1. Preheat oven to 375°F. Place hazelnuts on baking sheet; bake 8 minutes or until lightly browned. Quickly transfer nuts to clean dry dish towel. Fold towel over nuts; rub vigorously to remove as much of skins as possible. Using food processor, finely chop hazelnuts.

2. *Increase oven temperature to 450°F.* Place salmon in single layer in baking dish. Combine apple butter, mustard, thyme and pepper in small bowl. Brush onto salmon; top each steak with hazelnuts. Bake 14 to 16 minutes or until salmon begins to flake when tested with fork. Serve with herbed rice and steamed sugar snap peas, if desired. *Makes 4 servings*

Sweet and Sour Fish

In medium bowl, combine molasses, vinegar, 2 tablespoons cornstarch, pineapple juice, ketchup and soy sauce; blend well. Set aside. Coat swordfish with remaining ¼ cup cornstarch. In large skillet, heat 2 tablespoons oil. Stir-fry 5 minutes or until fish flakes easily with fork. Remove from skillet. Heat remaining 1 tablespoon oil in skillet. Stir-fry bell pepper and onions 2 minutes or until crisp-tender. Add molasses mixture; cook until thickened. Add fish and pineapple; cook until heated through. Serve over rice and garnish with tomatoes.

Makes 4 servings

⅓ cup GRANDMA'S® Molasses

¼ cup cider vinegar

¼ cup plus 2 tablespoons cornstarch, divided

2 tablespoons pineapple juice, reserved from chunks

2 tablespoons ketchup

2 tablespoons soy sauce

1 pound swordfish or red snapper, cut into 1-inch cubes

3 tablespoons vegetable oil, divided

1 green, red or yellow bell pepper, cut into strips

2 green onions, chopped

1 (8-ounce) can pineapple chunks in juice, drained, reserving 2 tablespoons juice

Hot cooked rice or noodles

Cherry tomatoes, cut into halves

Scallioned Scallops

¼ cup all-purpose flour
½ teaspoon dried thyme
½ teaspoon paprika
¼ teaspoon ground red pepper
1 pound scallops, rinsed and patted dry
2 teaspoons extra-virgin olive oil
¼ cup finely chopped green onion
¼ cup dry white wine or chicken broth
2 tablespoons lemon juice
2 tablespoons butter
½ teaspoon salt
2 tablespoons chopped fresh parsley leaves

1. In a shallow pan, such as a pie pan, combine flour, thyme, paprika and ground red pepper; blend well. Add scallops and toss until completely coated. Shake off excess flour; set aside.

2. Coat 12-inch nonstick skillet with cooking spray. Place over medium-high heat; add oil, tilting skillet to lightly coat bottom. Add scallops and cook 2 minutes; turn and cook 2 minutes longer or until opaque in center. Remove scallops from skillet and place on serving platter. Sprinkle green onion over scallops.

3. Return skillet to medium-high heat; add wine and lemon juice. Bring to a boil and continue boiling 1 minute or until reduced slightly, scraping bottom and sides. Remove from heat. Stir in butter and salt until melted. Pour over scallops and top with parsley.

Makes 4 servings

Stir-Fried Catfish with Cucumber Rice

1. Grate cucumber on medium side of grater into colander set over bowl; drain.

2. Combine water, rice, cucumber, green onions and white pepper in medium saucepan. Bring to a boil over medium heat. Cover; reduce heat to low. Cook about 20 minutes or until rice is tender and liquid is absorbed.

3. Heat oil in 12-inch nonstick skillet over high heat. Add catfish, ginger, garlic and sesame oil. Stir-fry 4 to 5 minutes or until catfish is just cooked. Add snow peas and bell pepper. Cover and cook 4 minutes.

4. Meanwhile, combine wine and cornstarch in small bowl; stir. Pour mixture over catfish mixture; cook and stir about 2 minutes or until sauce thickens. Serve over rice.   *Makes 4 servings*

Serving Suggestion: Serve with Egg Drop Soup made by stirring beaten egg into simmering fat-free, low-sodium chicken broth seasoned with your favorite fresh chopped herbs, such as cilantro. Complete the meal with chilled fresh seasonal fruit cups or a scoop of lemon sorbet.

1 cucumber
1¼ cups water
½ cup uncooked rice
4 green onions, thinly sliced
½ teaspoon white pepper
2 teaspoons canola oil
1 pound catfish fillets, cut into 1-inch chunks
1 teaspoon minced fresh ginger
1 clove garlic, minced
¼ teaspoon dark sesame oil
2 packages (6 ounces each) snow peas
1 red bell pepper, diced
¼ cup white wine or water
1 tablespoon cornstarch

Tuna Tomato Casserole

2 cans (6 ounces each) tuna packed in water, drained and flaked
1 cup mayonnaise
1 small onion, finely chopped
¼ teaspoon salt
¼ teaspoon black pepper
1 package (12 ounces) uncooked wide egg noodles
8 to 10 plum tomatoes, sliced ¼ inch thick
1 cup (4 ounces) shredded Cheddar or mozzarella cheese

1. Preheat oven to 375°F.

2. Combine tuna, mayonnaise, onion, salt and pepper in medium bowl; mix well.

3. Cook noodles according to package directions, just until tender. Drain noodles and return to saucepan. Add tuna mixture to noodles; stir until well blended.

4. Layer half of noodle mixture, half of tomatoes and half of cheese in 13×9-inch baking dish. Press down slightly. Repeat layers with remaining ingredients.

5. Bake 20 minutes or until cheese is melted and casserole is heated through.

Makes 6 servings

Noodles with Baby Shrimp

1. Place noodles in large bowl. Cover with hot tap water; let stand 10 to 15 minutes or just until softened. Drain noodles and cut into 5- or 6-inch pieces; set aside. Cut green onions into 1-inch pieces.

2. Heat wok over high heat about 1 minute. Drizzle vegetable oil into wok and heat 30 seconds. Add green onions; stir-fry 1 minute. Add mixed vegetables; stir-fry 2 minutes. Add broth; bring to a boil. Reduce heat to low; cover and cook about 5 minutes or until vegetables are crisp-tender.

3. Add shrimp to wok and cook just until thawed. Stir in noodles, soy sauce, sesame oil and pepper; stir-fry until heated through. Transfer to serving dish.

Makes 4 to 6 servings

1 package (about 4 ounces) bean thread noodles
3 green onions
1 tablespoon vegetable oil
1 package (16 ounces) frozen mixed vegetables (such as cauliflower, broccoli and carrots)
1 cup vegetable broth
8 ounces frozen cooked baby shrimp
1 tablespoon soy sauce
2 teaspoons dark sesame oil
¼ teaspoon black pepper

Cherry-Stuffed Perch Rolls

2 tablespoons butter, divided

¼ cup onion, finely chopped

¼ cup celery, finely chopped

1 cup sourdough or Italian bread, diced

½ cup dried sweetened cherries, chopped

¼ cup (about 2 ounces) shelled, salted pistachios, coarsely chopped

¼ teaspoon salt, divided

¼ teaspoon black pepper, divided

4 perch fillets (about 6 ounces each)

Lemon wedges (optional)

1. Preheat oven to 400°F. Grease 9-inch glass pie plate. Melt 1 tablespoon butter in medium skillet; add onion and celery. Cook and stir over medium-high heat 3 minutes. Add bread cubes, dried cherries, pistachios, ⅛ teaspoon salt and ⅛ teaspoon pepper. Toss and cook 1 minute. Remove from heat; let cool slightly.

2. Shape perch fillets into rolls and stand up in pie plate. Secure with wooden picks. Spoon generous ¼ cup cherry filling into center of each perch roll. Melt remaining 1 tablespoon butter; drizzle over perch. Sprinkle with remaining salt and pepper. Cover loosely with aluminum foil.

3. Bake 10 minutes. Remove foil; bake 5 minutes or until perch is firm, loses its translucent color and filling is lightly browned. Serve with lemon wedges, if desired.

Makes 4 servings

Smoked Salmon Hash Browns

1. Combine potatoes, salmon, onion, bell pepper and black pepper in bowl; toss gently to mix well.

2. Heat oil in large nonstick skillet over medium-high heat. Add potato mixture; spread to cover surface of skillet. Carefully pat down to avoid oil spatter.

3. Cook 5 minutes or until crisp and browned. Turn over in large pieces. Cook 2 to 3 minutes or until brown.

Makes 4 servings

3 cups frozen hash brown potatoes, thawed
2 pouches (3 ounces each) smoked Pacific salmon*
½ cup chopped onion
½ cup chopped bell pepper
¼ teaspoon black pepper
2 tablespoons vegetable oil

Smoked salmon in foil packages can be found in the canned fish section of the supermarket. Do not substitute lox or other fresh smoked salmon.

Fire Up the Grill

Shrimp on the Barbie

1 pound large raw shrimp, shelled and deveined
1 *each* red and yellow bell peppers, seeded and cut into 1-inch chunks
4 slices lime (optional)
½ cup prepared smoky-flavor barbecue sauce
2 tablespoons *French's®* Worcestershire Sauce
2 tablespoons *Frank's®* *RedHot®* Original Cayenne Pepper Sauce
1 clove garlic, minced

Thread shrimp, peppers and lime, if desired, alternately onto metal skewers. Combine barbecue sauce, Worcestershire, *Frank's RedHot* Sauce and garlic in small bowl; mix well. Brush on skewers.

Place skewers on grid, reserving remaining sauce mixture. Grill over hot coals 15 minutes or until shrimp turn pink, turning and basting often with sauce mixture. (Do not baste during last 5 minutes of cooking.) Serve warm.

Makes 4 servings

Prep Time: *10 minutes*
Cook Time: *15 minutes*

Grilled Swordfish with Mango Salsa

2 pounds swordfish steaks, cut 1 inch thick
1½ cups pineapple juice, divided
1 teaspoon minced fresh ginger, divided
2 mangoes, peeled and coarsely chopped
4 kiwi, peeled and chopped
1 cup pineapple chunks
1 tablespoon brown sugar
1 tablespoon grated orange peel

1. Place fish steaks in resealable food storage bag. Combine ¾ cup pineapple juice and ½ teaspoon ginger in small bowl. Pour over fish, turning to coat. Seal bag. Marinate in refrigerator about 2 hours, turning several times.

2. Combine remaining ¾ cup pineapple juice, remaining ½ teaspoon ginger, mangoes, kiwi, pineapple chunks, brown sugar and orange peel in medium bowl. Cover; refrigerate.

3. Prepare grill for direct cooking. Remove fish from marinade; discard marinade. Grill fish, covered, on oiled grid over medium-hot coals, 5 minutes on each side or until fish begins to flake when tested with fork. Or, arrange fish on rack of broiler pan sprayed with nonstick cooking spray. Broil, 4 inches from heat, 5 minutes on each side. Serve with mango salsa. *Makes 6 servings*

Teriyaki Salmon with Asian Slaw

1. Prepare grill for direct cooking. Spoon 2 tablespoons teriyaki sauce over fleshy sides of salmon. Let stand while preparing coleslaw mixture.

2. Combine coleslaw mix, snow peas and radishes in large bowl. Combine remaining 2 tablespoons teriyaki sauce, marmalade and sesame oil in small bowl. Add to coleslaw mixture; toss well.

3. Grill salmon, flesh side down, on oiled grid over medium coals, without turning, 6 to 10 minutes or until center is opaque.

4. Transfer coleslaw mixture to serving plates; top with salmon.

Makes 2 servings

4 tablespoons teriyaki sauce, divided
2 (5- to 6-ounce) boneless salmon fillets with skin (1 inch thick)
2½ cups coleslaw mix
1 cup fresh or frozen snow peas, cut lengthwise into thin strips
½ cup thinly sliced radishes
2 tablespoons orange marmalade
1 teaspoon dark sesame oil

Fire Up the Grill

Jamaican Shrimp & Pineapple Kabobs

½ cup prepared jerk sauce

¼ cup pineapple preserves

2 tablespoons minced fresh chives

1 pound large raw shrimp, peeled and deveined

½ medium pineapple, peeled, cored and cut into 1-inch cubes

2 large red, green or yellow bell peppers, cut into 1-inch squares

1. Combine jerk sauce, preserves and chives in small bowl; mix well. Reserve half of sauce mixture; set aside. Thread shrimp, pineapple and peppers onto 4 skewers; brush with remaining jerk sauce mixture.

2. Grill kabobs over medium-hot coals 6 to 10 minutes or until shrimp are pink and opaque, turning once. Serve with reserved jerk sauce mixture for dipping.

Makes 4 servings

Time-Saving Tip: Purchase pineapple already trimmed and cored in the produce section of your local supermarket.

Prep and Cook Time: *25 minutes*

Blackened Sea Bass

1. Prepare grill for direct cooking using hardwood charcoal.

2. Meanwhile, combine paprika, garlic salt, thyme and white, red and black peppers in small bowl; mix well. Set aside. Melt butter in small saucepan over medium heat. Pour melted butter into pie plate or shallow bowl. Cool slightly.

3. Dip sea bass into melted butter, evenly coating both sides. Sprinkle both sides of sea bass evenly with paprika mixture.

4. Place sea bass on oiled grid. (Fire will flare up when sea bass is placed on grid, but will subside when grill is covered.) Grill sea bass, covered, over hot coals 4 to 6 minutes or until sea bass is blackened and begins to flake when tested with fork, turning halfway through grilling time. *Makes 4 servings*

Hardwood charcoal*
2 teaspoons paprika
1 teaspoon garlic salt
1 teaspoon dried thyme
¼ teaspoon white pepper
¼ teaspoon ground red pepper
¼ teaspoon black pepper
3 tablespoons butter
4 skinless sea bass or catfish fillets (4 ounces each)

Hardwood charcoal takes longer than regular charcoal to become hot, but results in a hotter fire. A hot fire is necessary to create a flavorful char crust and cook fish quickly. If hardwood charcoal is not available, scatter dry untreated hardwood (such as mesquite or hickory chunks) over hot coals to increase the heat.

Mustard-Grilled Red Snapper

½ cup Dijon mustard
1 tablespoon red wine
    vinegar
1 teaspoon ground red
    pepper
4 red snapper fillets (about
    6 ounces each)
    Fresh parsley sprigs and
    red peppercorns
    (optional)

1. Spray grid with nonstick cooking spray. Prepare grill for direct cooking.

2. Combine mustard, vinegar and red pepper in small bowl; mix well. Coat fish thoroughly with mustard mixture.

3. Place fish on grid. Grill, covered, over medium-high heat 8 minutes, turning halfway through grilling time, or until fish begins to flake when tested with fork. Garnish with parsley sprigs and red peppercorns, if desired.

Makes 4 servings

Grilled Swordfish Sicilian Style

3 tablespoons extra-virgin
    olive oil
1 clove garlic, minced
2 tablespoons lemon juice
¾ teaspoon salt
⅛ teaspoon black pepper
3 tablespoons capers,
    drained
1 tablespoon chopped
    fresh oregano or basil
1½ pounds swordfish steaks
    (¾ inch thick)
    Lemon slices (optional)

1. Prepare grill for direct cooking.

2. Heat olive oil in small saucepan over low heat; add garlic. Cook 1 minute. Remove from heat; cool slightly. Whisk in lemon juice, salt and pepper until salt is dissolved. Stir in capers and oregano.

3. Place swordfish on oiled grid over medium heat. Grill 7 to 8 minutes, turning once, or until fish is opaque in center. Serve fish with lemon juice mixture drizzled over top. Garnish with lemon slices, if desired.

Makes 4 to 6 servings

Hot Shrimp with Cool Salsa

1. To make marinade, combine salsa, 2 tablespoons lime juice, honey, garlic and hot pepper sauce in small bowl. Thread shrimp onto skewers. Brush shrimp with marinade; set aside.

2. To make salsa, combine remaining 2 tablespoons lime juice, melon, cucumber, parsley, green onion, sugar, oil and salt in medium bowl; mix well.

3. Grill shrimp over medium coals 4 to 5 minutes or until shrimp are pink and opaque, turning once. Serve with salsa.   *Makes 4 servings*

¼ **cup salsa**
4 **tablespoons fresh lime juice, divided**
1 **teaspoon honey**
1 **clove garlic, minced**
2 **drops hot pepper sauce**
1 **pound large raw shrimp, peeled and deveined, tails intact**
1 **cup finely diced honeydew melon**
½ **cup finely diced unpeeled cucumber**
2 **tablespoons minced fresh parsley**
1 **green onion, finely chopped**
1½ **teaspoons sugar**
1 **teaspoon olive oil**
¼ **teaspoon salt**

Szechuan Tuna Steaks

4 tuna steaks (6 ounces each), cut 1 inch thick
¼ cup dry sherry or sake
¼ cup soy sauce
1 tablespoon dark sesame oil
1 teaspoon hot chili oil *or* ¼ teaspoon red pepper flakes
1 clove garlic, minced
3 tablespoons chopped fresh cilantro

1. Place tuna in single layer in large shallow glass dish. Combine sherry, soy sauce, sesame oil, hot chili oil and garlic in small bowl. Reserve ¼ cup soy sauce mixture at room temperature. Pour remaining soy sauce mixture over tuna. Cover; marinate in refrigerator 40 minutes, turning once.

2. Spray grid with nonstick cooking spray. Prepare grill for direct grilling.

3. Drain tuna, discarding marinade. Place tuna on grid. Grill, uncovered, over medium-hot coals 6 minutes or until tuna is opaque, but still feels somewhat soft in center,* turning halfway through grilling time. Transfer tuna to carving board. Cut each tuna steak into thin slices; fan out slices onto serving plates. Drizzle tuna slices with reserved soy sauce mixture; sprinkle with cilantro.

Makes 4 servings

Tuna becomes dry and tough if overcooked. Cook it as if it were beef.

Lemon Herbed Seafood Kabobs

In small nonstick skillet, heat oil; add onion, rosemary, thyme and lemon peel. Cook over low heat 1 to 2 minutes to infuse oil. Remove from heat; add lemon juice and salt. Cool. Pour oil mixture over fish in resealable plastic food storage bag. Seal bag and marinate in refrigerator 1 hour or longer, turning occasionally. To make kabobs, arrange drained fish, bell pepper and mushrooms alternately on four 10-inch metal skewers. Lightly brush mushrooms, peppers and fish with small amount of additional oil. Barbecue on grill 4 to 6 inches above glowing coals or on medium heat of gas barbecue 12 to 14 minutes or until fish is opaque and flakes easily with fork (turning about 3 times). Or, broil 4 inches from heat 12 to 14 minutes. *Makes 4 servings*

2 tablespoons vegetable oil
2 tablespoons finely chopped onion
¼ teaspoon dried rosemary
¼ teaspoon dried thyme
  Grated peel of ½ SUNKIST® lemon
  Juice of 1 SUNKIST® lemon (3 tablespoons)
¼ teaspoon salt
1 pound halibut or shark steak, cut into 1-inch cubes *or* 1 pound sea scallops (16 to 20)
12 (1-inch square) pieces red or green bell pepper
12 medium button mushrooms

Spicy Margarita Shrimp

⅔ cup *Frank's® RedHot® Chile 'n Lime™ Hot Sauce*
¼ cup olive oil
2 tablespoons lime juice
1 teaspoon grated lime zest
2 teaspoons minced garlic
1½ pounds jumbo raw shrimp, shelled and deveined
1 (16 ounce) jar mild chunky salsa
2 tablespoons minced fresh cilantro
2 red or orange bell peppers, cut into chunks

1. Whisk together *Chile 'n Lime™* Hot Sauce, oil, lime juice, zest and garlic. Place shrimp into resealable plastic bag. Pour ⅔ cup marinade over shrimp. Seal bag; marinate in refrigerator 30 minutes.

2. Combine remaining marinade with salsa and cilantro in bowl; set aside.

3. Place shrimp and bell pepper chunks on metal skewers. Grill over medium-high direct heat about 8 minutes until shrimp turn pink. Serve with spicy salsa on the side.   *Makes 4 to 6 servings*

Tip: To make Mesa Grill BBQ Sauce, add ½ cup *Frank's® Redhot® Chile 'n Lime™* Hot Sauce to 1 cup *Cattlemen's®* Authentic Smoke House Barbecue Sauce.

Prep Time: *10 minutes*
Cook Time: *8 minutes*
Marinate Time: *30 minutes*

Salmon with Warm Mango Salsa

1. Prepare grill for direct cooking.

2. Rinse salmon under cold running water; pat dry with paper towels. Cut salmon into 4 serving-size pieces. Place one piece salmon, skin side down, on each sheet of foil. Combine paprika and red pepper in small bowl. Rub on tops of salmon pieces.

3. Toss together mangoes, bell pepper, jalapeño, parsley and juice concentrate. Spoon onto salmon pieces.

4. Double-fold sides and ends of foil to seal packets, leaving head space for heat circulation. Place on baking sheet.

5. Slide packets off baking sheet onto grid. Grill, covered, over medium-high coals 9 to 11 minutes or until fish begins to flake when tested with fork. Carefully open one end of each packet to allow steam to escape. Open packets and transfer to serving plates. *Makes 4 servings*

1¼ pounds salmon fillet, about 1 inch thick
½ teaspoon paprika
⅛ teaspoon ground red pepper
4 sheets (18×12 inches) heavy-duty foil, lightly sprayed with nonstick cooking spray
2 medium mangoes, peeled, cut into ¾-inch pieces
½ medium red bell pepper, chopped
1 jalapeño pepper,* seeded and finely chopped
2 tablespoons chopped fresh parsley
1 tablespoon frozen orange-pineapple juice concentrate, thawed

Jalapeño peppers can sting and irritate the skin, so wear rubber gloves when handling peppers and do not touch your eyes.

Grilled Garlic-Pepper Shrimp

⅓ cup olive oil
2 tablespoons lemon juice
1 teaspoon garlic-pepper seasoning
20 jumbo raw shrimp, peeled and deveined
Lemon wedges (optional)

1. Spray grid with nonstick cooking spray. Prepare grill for direct cooking.

2. Meanwhile, combine oil, lemon juice and garlic pepper in large resealable food storage bag; add shrimp. Marinate 20 to 30 minutes in refrigerator, turning bag once.

3. Thread 5 shrimp onto each of 4 skewers;* discard marinade. Grill on grid over medium heat 6 minutes or until pink and opaque. Serve with lemon wedges, if desired. *Makes 4 servings*

If using wooden skewers, soak in water 20 minutes before using to prevent burning.

Lobster Tails with Tasty Butters

1. Prepare grill for direct cooking. Prepare choice of butter mixtures.

2. Rinse lobster tails in cold water. Butterfly tails by cutting lengthwise through centers of hard top shells and meat. Cut to, but not through, bottoms of shells. Press shell halves of tails apart with fingers. Brush lobster meat with butter mixture.

3. Place tails on grid, meat side down. Grill, uncovered, over medium-high heat 4 minutes. Turn tails meat side up. Brush with butter mixture; grill 4 to 5 minutes or until lobster meat turns opaque.

4. Heat remaining butter mixture, stirring occasionally. Serve butter mixture for dipping.

Makes 4 servings

Tasty Butters

Hot & Spicy Butter
- ⅓ cup butter or margarine, melted
- 1 tablespoon chopped onion
- 2 to 3 teaspoons hot pepper sauce
- 1 teaspoon dried thyme
- ¼ teaspoon ground allspice

Scallion Butter
- ⅓ cup butter or margarine, melted
- 1 tablespoon finely chopped green onion tops
- 1 tablespoon lemon juice
- 1 teaspoon grated lemon peel
- ¼ teaspoon black pepper

Chili-Mustard Butter
- ⅓ cup butter or margarine, melted
- 1 tablespoon chopped onion
- 1 tablespoon Dijon mustard
- 1 teaspoon chili powder

For each butter sauce, combine ingredients in small bowl.

Hot & Spicy Butter,
Scallion Butter or
Chili-Mustard Butter
(recipes follow)
4 fresh or thawed frozen
lobster tails (about
5 ounces each)

Seafood Kabobs

1 pound large raw shrimp, peeled and deveined

10 ounces skinless swordfish or halibut steaks, cut 1 inch thick

2 tablespoons honey mustard

2 teaspoons fresh lemon juice

8 (12-inch) metal skewers

8 slices bacon

Lemon wedges and fresh herbs (optional)

1. Spray grid with nonstick cooking spray. Prepare grill for direct cooking.

2. Place shrimp in shallow glass dish. Cut swordfish into 1-inch cubes; add to dish. Combine mustard and lemon juice in small bowl. Pour over seafood; toss lightly to coat.

3. Pierce one 12-inch metal skewer through 1 end of bacon slice. Add 1 shrimp. Pierce skewer through bacon slice again, wrapping bacon slice around 1 side of shrimp.

4. Add 1 piece swordfish. Pierce bacon slice again, wrapping bacon around opposite side of swordfish. Continue adding seafood and wrapping with bacon, pushing ingredients to middle of skewer until end of bacon slice is reached. Repeat with 7 more skewers. Brush any remaining mustard mixture over skewers.

5. Place skewers on grid. Grill, covered, over medium heat 8 to 10 minutes or until shrimp are pink and opaque and swordfish begins to flake when tested with fork, turning halfway through grilling time. Garnish as desired.

Makes 4 servings

Grilled Fish with Chili-Corn Salsa

1. Combine corn, tomato, green onions, green chiles, cilantro, lime juice, 2 teaspoons oil and cumin in small bowl; mix well. Add salt and pepper to taste. Let stand at room temperature 30 minutes for flavors to blend.

2. Prepare grill for direct cooking. Brush fish with remaining 2 teaspoons oil; season with salt and pepper. Place fish on oiled grid 4 to 6 inches over medium-high heat. Cook, turning once, 4 to 5 minutes on each side or until fish begins to flake when tested with fork. Serve with salsa.   *Makes 4 servings*

1 cup cooked corn
1 large tomato, seeded and diced
¼ cup thinly sliced green onions with tops
¼ cup canned diced green chiles
1 tablespoon coarsely chopped fresh cilantro
1 tablespoon lime juice
4 teaspoons olive oil, divided
⅛ teaspoon ground cumin
Salt and black pepper
1½ pounds firm-textured fish steaks or fillets such as halibut, salmon, sea bass or swordfish, each 1 inch thick

Surf & Turf Kabobs

1 pound beef tenderloin, cut into 1¼-inch chunks
12 jumbo raw shrimp, peeled and deveined, tails intact
1 medium onion, cut into 12 wedges
1 red or yellow bell pepper, cut into 1-inch chunks
⅓ cup unsalted butter, melted
3 tablespoons lemon juice
3 cloves garlic, minced
2 teaspoons paprika or smoked paprika
1 teaspoon salt
¼ teaspoon black pepper or ground red pepper
Lemon wedges

1. Spray grid with nonstick cooking spray. Prepare grill for direct cooking. Alternately thread beef, shrimp, onion and bell pepper onto 12-inch metal skewers. (Skewer shrimp through ends to form "C" shape for even cooking.)

2. Combine remaining ingredients, except lemon wedges; transfer to small saucepan or metal bowl.

3. Place butter sauce on edge of grill until butter melts; stir well. Place skewers on grid over medium coals; brush with half of butter mixture. Grill 5 minutes; turn and brush with remaining butter sauce. Continue grilling 5 to 6 minutes or until shrimp are pink and opaque (beef will be medium-rare to medium doneness). Serve with lemon wedges. *Makes 4 servings*

Grilled Red Snapper with Avocado-Papaya Salsa

1. Prepare grill for direct grilling. Combine coriander, paprika, salt and red pepper in small bowl or cup; mix well.

2. Brush oil over fish. Sprinkle 2½ teaspoons spice mixture over fish fillets; set aside remaining spice mixture. Place fish on oiled grid over medium-hot heat. Grill 5 minutes per side or until fish is opaque in center.

3. Meanwhile, combine avocado, papaya, cilantro, lime juice and remaining spice mixture in medium bowl; mix well. Serve fish with salsa and garnish with lime wedges. *Makes 4 servings*

1 teaspoon ground
  coriander
1 teaspoon paprika
¾ teaspoon salt
⅛ to ¼ teaspoon ground
  red pepper
1 tablespoon olive oil
4 skinless red snapper or
  halibut fillets (5 to
  7 ounces each)
½ cup diced ripe avocado
½ cup diced ripe papaya
2 tablespoons chopped
  fresh cilantro
1 tablespoon fresh lime
  juice
4 lime wedges

Fire Up the Grill

Grilled Chinese Salmon

3 tablespoons soy sauce
2 tablespoons dry sherry
2 cloves garlic, minced
1 pound salmon fillets or
    steaks
2 tablespoons finely
    chopped fresh cilantro

1. Combine soy sauce, sherry and garlic in shallow dish. Add salmon; turn to coat. Cover and refrigerate at least 30 minutes or up to 2 hours.

2. Drain salmon; reserve marinade. Arrange fillets skin side down on oiled grid over hot coals. Grill 5 to 6 inches from heat 10 minutes. Baste with reserved marinade after 5 minutes of grilling; discard any remaining marinade. Sprinkle with cilantro.

Makes 4 servings

Grilled Shrimp Salad with Hot Bacon Vinaigrette

1. Cook bacon until crisp in medium skillet. Whisk in salad dressing, mustard and water; keep warm over very low heat.

2. Place salad greens, bell peppers, tomatoes and pine nuts in large bowl; toss. Arrange on salad plates.

3. Cook shrimp on electric grill pan or barbecue grill 3 minutes until pink. Arrange on salads, dividing evenly. Serve with dressing.   *Makes 4 servings*

Prep Time: *10 minutes*
Cook Time: *5 minutes*

4 strips bacon, chopped
½ cup prepared Italian or vinaigrette salad dressing
⅓ cup *French's®* Honey Dijon Mustard or *French's®* Honey Mustard
2 tablespoons water
8 cups mixed salad greens
1 cup diced yellow bell peppers
1 cup halved cherry tomatoes
½ cup pine nuts
1 pound jumbo or extra large raw shrimp, shelled with tails intact

Fire Up the Grill

Pineapple Salsa Topped Halibut

Pineapple Salsa
¾ **cup diced fresh pineapple** *or* **1 can (8 ounces) unsweetened pineapple chunks, drained**
2 **tablespoons finely chopped red bell pepper**
2 **tablespoons chopped fresh cilantro**
2 **teaspoons vegetable oil**
1 **teaspoon minced fresh ginger**
1 **teaspoon minced jalapeño pepper***

Halibut
4 **halibut or swordfish steaks or fillets (6 ounces each)**
1 **tablespoon garlic-flavored olive oil**
¼ **teaspoon salt**

*Jalapeño peppers can sting and irritate the skin, so wear rubber gloves when handling peppers and do not touch your eyes.

1. For salsa, combine pineapple, bell pepper, cilantro, vegetable oil, ginger and jalapeño pepper in small bowl; mix well. Cover; refrigerate until ready to serve.

2. Spray grid with nonstick cooking spray. Prepare grill for direct cooking. Brush halibut with olive oil; sprinkle with salt.

3. Grill halibut on uncovered grill over medium-hot coals 8 minutes or until fish begins to flake when tested with fork, turning once. Serve halibut with pineapple salsa.
Makes 4 servings

Prep Time: *20 minutes*
Cook Time: *11 minutes*

Grilled Lobster, Shrimp and Calamari Seviche

1. To make marinade, combine orange juice, lime juice, tequila, jalapeños, cilantro and honey in medium glass bowl.

2. Measure ¼ cup marinade into small glass bowl; stir in cumin and oil. Set aside. Refrigerate remaining marinade.

3. Prepare grill for direct grilling.

4. Bring 1 quart water to a boil in 2-quart saucepan over high heat. Add squid; cook 30 seconds or until opaque. Drain. Rinse under cold water; drain. Add squid to refrigerated marinade.

5. Thread shrimp onto metal skewers. Brush shrimp and lobster tails with reserved ¼ cup marinade.

6. Place shrimp on grid. Grill shrimp on uncovered grill over medium-hot coals 2 to 3 minutes per side or until shrimp turn pink and opaque. Remove shrimp from skewers; add to squid. Place lobster on grid. Grill 5 minutes per side or until meat turns opaque and is cooked through. Slice lobster meat into ¼-inch-thick slices; add to squid and shrimp mixture.

7. Refrigerate at least 2 hours or overnight.

Makes 6 appetizer servings

¾ **cup fresh orange juice**
⅓ **cup fresh lime juice**
2 **tablespoons tequila**
2 **jalapeño peppers,***
seeded and minced
2 **tablespoons chopped**
fresh cilantro
1 **teaspoon honey**
1 **teaspoon ground cumin**
1 **teaspoon olive oil**
10 **squid, cleaned and cut**
into rings and tentacles
½ **pound medium raw**
shrimp, peeled and
deveined
2 **lobster tails (8 ounces**
each), meat removed
and shells discarded

*Jalapeño peppers can sting and irritate the skin, so wear rubber gloves when handling peppers and do not touch your eyes.

Thai Seafood Kabobs with Spicy Peanut Rice

1¼ cups UNCLE BEN'S® ORIGINAL CONVERTED® Brand Rice

1 pound medium raw shrimp, peeled and deveined, with tails intact

½ pound bay scallops

¼ cup soy sauce

2 tablespoons sesame oil

1 large red bell pepper, cut into 1-inch squares

6 green onions with tops, cut into 1-inch pieces

½ cup prepared Thai peanut sauce*

½ cup chopped peanuts

*Thai peanut sauce can be found in the Asian section of large supermarket.

1. Cook rice according to package directions.

2. Meanwhile, place shrimp and scallops in medium bowl. Combine soy sauce and sesame oil; pour half of mixture over shellfish, tossing to coat. Let stand 15 minutes. Reserve remaining soy sauce mixture for basting.

3. Alternately thread shrimp, scallops, bell pepper and green onions onto twelve 12-inch metal skewers. Brush with half the reserved soy sauce mixture. Spoon Thai peanut sauce over each skewer, coating evenly. Grill or broil 8 minutes or until shrimp are pink and scallops are opaque, turning and brushing once with remaining soy sauce mixture and Thai peanut sauce.

4. Stir peanuts into cooked rice; place on serving platter. Top with seafood kabobs. Serve immediately. *Makes 6 servings*

Serving Suggestion: Garnish with minced fresh cilantro, if desired.

Grilled Sea Bass with Ripe Olive 'n Caper Salsa

Preheat grill or broiler. Combine all ingredients except sea bass and olive oil in large bowl. Mix well. Adjust seasoning with salt and pepper. Cover and chill. Brush both sides of fillets with olive oil and season with salt and pepper. Broil or grill until fish is firm to the touch, about 5 minutes on each side. Serve each fillet with about ¼ cup of Ripe Olive 'n Caper Salsa. *Makes 8 servings*

*Favorite recipe from **California Olive Industry***

1 cup sliced California Ripe Olives
½ cup seeded, diced Roma tomatoes
½ cup chopped oil-packed sun-dried tomatoes
¼ cup minced red onion
¼ cup chopped fresh basil
3 tablespoons capers
2 tablespoons chopped fresh parsley
2 tablespoons Balsamic-style vinaigrette dressing
1 teaspoon minced garlic
8 (6-ounce) sea bass or other white fish fillets
Olive oil

Moroccan Swordfish

1. Place swordfish in single layer in medium shallow dish. Combine lemon juice, vinegar, garlic-flavored oil, ginger, paprika, cumin, chili oil, salt, coriander and pepper in small bowl. Pour over swordfish; turn to coat both sides. Cover; refrigerate 40 minutes, turning once.

2. Prepare grill for direct cooking. Discard marinade; grill swordfish, uncovered, over medium-hot coals 8 to 10 minutes or until swordfish is opaque and begins to flake when tested with fork, turning once. Serve with couscous. *Makes 4 servings*

4 swordfish steaks (4 ounces each), about 1 inch thick
1 tablespoon fresh lemon juice
1 tablespoon apple cider vinegar
2½ teaspoons garlic-flavored olive oil
1 teaspoon ground ginger
1 teaspoon paprika
½ teaspoon ground cumin
½ teaspoon hot chili oil
¼ teaspoon salt
¼ teaspoon ground coriander
⅛ teaspoon black pepper
2⅔ cups hot cooked couscous

Grilled Tuna Niçoise with Citrus Marinade

Citrus Marinade (recipe
  follows)
1 tuna steak (about
  1 pound)
2 cups fresh green beans,
  trimmed and halved
4 cups romaine lettuce
  leaves, washed and
  torn
8 small red potatoes,
  cooked and quartered
1 cup chopped seeded
  fresh tomato
4 cooked egg whites,
  chopped
¼ cup red onion slices
2 teaspoons chopped black
  olives
  Prepared salad dressing
  (optional)

1. Prepare Citrus Marinade; combine with tuna in large resealable food storage bag. Seal bag; turn to coat. Marinate in refrigerator 1 hour, turning occasionally.* Drain tuna; discard marinade.

2. Spray cold grid of grill with nonstick cooking spray. Prepare coals for direct grilling.

3. Place tuna on grid, 4 inches from hot coals. Grill 8 to 10 minutes or until tuna begins to flake when tested with fork, turning once during grilling. (Or, place tuna on rack of broiler pan coated with nonstick cooking spray. Broil 4 inches from heat, 8 to 10 minutes or until tuna begins to flake when tested with fork, turning once during broiling.) Slice tuna into ¼-inch-thick slices; set aside.

4. Place 2 cups water in large saucepan; bring to a boil over high heat. Add beans; cook 2 minutes. Drain; rinse with cold water and drain again.

5. Place lettuce on large serving platter. Arrange tuna, beans, potatoes, tomato, egg whites and onion on lettuce. Sprinkle each serving with olives. Serve with salad dressing, if desired.   *Makes 4 servings*

Marinate in refrigerator 1 hour for each inch of thickness.

Citrus Marinade

  ½ **cup fresh lime juice**
  ¼ **cup vegetable oil**
  2 **green onions, chopped**
  1 **teaspoon dried tarragon**
  ¼ **teaspoon garlic powder**
  ¼ **teaspoon black pepper**

Blend all ingredients in small bowl.

Fire Up the Grill

Grilled Tropical Shrimp

1. Stir together barbecue sauce and pineapple juice. Set aside.

2. Cut each nectarine into 6 wedges. Thread shrimp, nectarines and onion wedges onto 4 long metal skewers.

3. Spray grill grid with nonstick cooking spray. Prepare grill for direct grilling. Grill skewers over medium coals 4 to 5 minutes or until shrimp are pink and opaque, turning once and brushing frequently with barbecue sauce.

Makes 2 servings

¼ cup barbecue sauce
2 tablespoons pineapple juice or orange juice
2 medium firm nectarines
10 ounces medium raw shrimp, peeled and deveined, tails intact
1 yellow onion, cut into 8 wedges, *or* 6 green onions, cut into 2-inch lengths

Fire Up the Grill

Scallop Kabobs

1 pound Florida calico scallops, fresh or frozen

2 cups cherry tomatoes

2 cups small mushrooms

1 can (13½ ounces) pineapple chunks, drained

1 green pepper, cut into 1-inch squares

¼ cup vegetable oil

¼ cup lemon juice

¼ cup chopped fresh parsley

¼ cup soy sauce

½ teaspoon salt

⅛ teaspoon black pepper

Thaw scallops, if frozen. Rinse scallops with cold running water to remove any remaining shell particles. Place tomatoes, mushrooms, pineapple, green pepper and scallops in a bowl. Combine oil, lemon juice, parsley, soy sauce, salt and black pepper. Pour sauce over scallop mixture and let stand for 30 minutes, stirring occasionally. Using long skewers, alternate scallops, tomatoes, mushrooms, pineapple and green pepper until skewers are filled. Cook about 4 minutes over moderately hot coals. Baste with sauce. Turn and cook for 3 to 4 minutes longer.

Makes 6 servings

Favorite recipe from **Florida Department of Agriculture and Consumer Services, Bureau of Seafood and Aquaculture**

Fire Up the Grill

Grilled Five-Spice Fish with Garlic Spinach

1. Combine lime peel, lime juice, ginger, 1 teaspoon oil, five-spice powder, sugar, salt and pepper in 2-quart dish. Add salmon; turn to coat. Cover; refrigerate 2 to 3 hours.

2. Combine spinach, garlic and remaining 1 teaspoon oil in 3-quart microwavable dish; toss. Cover; microwave on HIGH 2 minutes or until spinach is wilted. Drain; keep warm.

3. Meanwhile, prepare grill for direct cooking.

4. Remove salmon from marinade and place on oiled grid. Brush salmon with marinade. Grill salmon, covered, over medium-hot coals 4 minutes. Turn salmon; brush with marinade and grill 4 minutes or until salmon begins to flake with fork. Discard remaining marinade. Serve fish over bed of spinach.

Makes 4 servings

1½ teaspoons grated lime peel
3 tablespoons fresh lime juice
4 teaspoons minced fresh ginger
2 teaspoons vegetable oil, divided
½ to 1 teaspoon Chinese five-spice powder*
½ teaspoon sugar
½ teaspoon salt
⅛ teaspoon black pepper
1 pound salmon steaks
½ pound fresh baby spinach leaves (about 8 cups lightly packed), washed
2 cloves garlic, pressed

*Chinese five-spice powder is a blend of cinnamon, cloves, fennel seed, anise and Szechuan peppercorns. It is available in most supermarkets and at Asian grocery stores.

Italian Mixed Seafood

½ pound large raw shrimp, peeled and deveined

½ pound sea scallops

1 small zucchini, cut into ½-inch pieces

1 small red bell pepper, cut into ½-inch pieces

1 small red onion, cut into wedges

12 large mushrooms

1 bottle (8 ounces) Italian salad dressing

2 teaspoons dried Italian seasoning, divided

1½ cups uncooked brown rice

2 cans (about 14 ounces each) chicken broth

1. Place shrimp, scallops, zucchini, bell pepper, onion, mushrooms, salad dressing and 1 teaspoon Italian seasoning in large resealable food storage bag. Close bag securely, turning to coat. Marinate in refrigerator 30 minutes, turning after 15 minutes.

2. Meanwhile, place rice, chicken broth and remaining 1 teaspoon Italian seasoning in medium saucepan over high heat. Bring to a boil; cover and reduce heat to low. Simmer 35 minutes or until liquid is absorbed.

3. Meanwhile, prepare grill for direct cooking.

4. Drain seafood and vegetables; reserve marinade. Place seafood and vegetables in lightly oiled grill basket or on vegetable grilling grid. Grill, covered, over medium-high heat 4 to 5 minutes; turn and baste with marinade. Discard remaining marinade. Grill 4 to 5 minutes or until shrimp are pink and opaque. Serve seafood and vegetables over rice. *Makes 4 to 6 servings*

Grilled Swordfish with Pineapple Salsa

1. Combine lime juice and garlic on plate. Dip swordfish in juice; sprinkle with chili powder.

2. Spray cold grid with nonstick cooking spray. Adjust grid 4 to 6 inches above heat. Preheat grill to medium-high heat. Grill fish, covered, 2 to 3 minutes. Turn over; grill 1 to 2 minutes more or until just opaque in center but still very moist. Top each serving with Pineapple Salsa.

Makes 4 servings

Pineapple Salsa

- ½ **cup finely chopped fresh pineapple**
- ¼ **cup finely chopped red bell pepper**
- 1 **green onion, thinly sliced**
- 2 **tablespoons lime juice**
- ½ **jalapeño pepper,* seeded and minced**
- 1 **tablespoon chopped fresh cilantro or fresh basil**

*Jalapeño peppers can sting and irritate the skin, so wear rubber gloves when handling peppers and do not touch your eyes.

Combine all ingredients in small nonreactive bowl. Serve at room temperature.

Makes 4 servings

1 **tablespoon lime juice**
2 **cloves garlic, minced**
4 **swordfish steaks**
    (**5 ounces each**)
½ **teaspoon chili powder or black pepper**
  Pineapple Salsa (recipe follows)

Deep-Fried Favorites

Shrimp Toast

12 large raw shrimp, peeled and deveined, tails intact

1 egg

2 tablespoons plus 1½ teaspoons cornstarch

¼ teaspoon salt
Dash black pepper

3 slices white sandwich bread, crusts removed, quartered

1 hard-cooked egg yolk, cut into ½-inch pieces

1 slice (1 ounce) cooked ham, cut into ½-inch pieces

1 green onion, finely chopped
Vegetable oil for frying

1. Cut deep slit down back of each shrimp; press gently with fingers to flatten.

2. Beat egg, cornstarch, salt and pepper in large bowl until blended. Add shrimp; toss to coat well.

3. Drain each shrimp and press, cut side down, into each piece of bread. Brush small amount of leftover egg mixture onto each shrimp.

4. Place one piece each of egg yolk and ham and scant ¼ teaspoon green onion on top of each shrimp.

5. Heat oil in wok or large skillet over medium-high heat to 375°F. Add three or four bread pieces at a time; cook 1 to 2 minutes on each side or until golden. Drain on paper towels. Garnish as desired. *Makes 12 servings*

Note: To keep shrimp from flattening during cooking, spoon hot oil in skillet over the shrimp toasts until cooked through instead of turning them over.

Crusty Hot Pan-Fried Fish

1½ cups all-purpose flour
3½ teaspoons Chef Paul
    Prudhomme's Seafood
    Magic®, divided
1 cup milk
1 large egg, beaten
6 fish fillets (4 ounces
    each), speckled trout
    or drum or your
    favorite fish
    Vegetable oil for frying

In flat pan, combine flour and 2 teaspoons of the Seafood Magic®. In separate pan, combine milk and egg until well blended. Season fillets by sprinkling about ¼ teaspoon of the Seafood Magic® on each. In large skillet, heat about ¼ inch oil over medium heat until hot. Meanwhile, coat each fillet with seasoned flour, shake off excess and coat well with milk mixture; then, just before frying, coat fillets once more with flour, shaking off excess. Fry fillets in hot oil until golden brown, 1 to 2 minutes per side. Drain on paper towels and serve immediately on heated serving plates. *Makes 6 servings*

Deep-Fried Favorites

Magic Fried Oysters

Place oysters and oyster liquor in large bowl. Add 2 tablespoons of the Seafood Magic® to oysters, stirring well. In medium bowl, combine flour, corn flour, cornmeal and the remaining 1 tablespoon Seafood Magic®. Heat 2 inches or more of oil in deep-fryer or large saucepan to 375°F. Drain oysters and then use a slotted spoon to toss them lightly and quickly in seasoned flour mixture (so oysters don't produce excess moisture, which cakes the flour); shake off excess flour and carefully slip each oyster into hot oil. Fry in single layer in batches just until crispy and golden brown, 1 to 1½ minutes; do not overcook. (Adjust heat as needed to maintain temperature at about 375°F.) Drain on paper towels and serve. *Makes 6 servings*

6 dozen medium to large shucked oysters in their liquor (about 3 pounds)
3 tablespoons Chef Paul Prudhomme's Seafood Magic®, divided
1 cup all-purpose flour
1 cup corn flour
1 cup cornmeal
Vegetable oil for frying

Deep-Fried Favorites

Stuffed Vegetable Tempura

½ cup all-purpose flour
2 tablespoons plus
    ½ teaspoon
    cornstarch, divided
1 teaspoon baking powder
¼ teaspoon salt
¾ cup cold water
1 egg, separated
1 pound large raw shrimp,
    peeled and deveined
1 tablespoon soy sauce
2 teaspoons sesame oil
4 cups vegetable oil
1 zucchini, diagonally cut
    into ½-inch-thick slices
8 button mushrooms,
    stems removed
1 red bell pepper, cut into
    wedges
1 green bell pepper, cut
    into wedges
    Prepared Asian dipping
    sauce

1. To prepare batter, place flour, 2 tablespoons cornstarch, baking powder and salt in medium bowl; mix well with wire whisk. Make well in center and whisk in water until batter is consistency of pancake batter with small lumps.

2. Add egg white to batter; whisk until blended. Cover and refrigerate 30 minutes.

3. Meanwhile, place yolk in food processor. Add shrimp, soy sauce, sesame oil and remaining ½ teaspoon cornstarch to food processor. Process until shrimp is chopped to a paste. Place shrimp paste in small bowl; cover and refrigerate.

4. Heat vegetable oil in wok over medium-high heat until oil registers 375°F on deep-fry thermometer. Spread about 1½ to 2 teaspoons shrimp paste on 1 side of 8 zucchini slices and stuff remaining paste into mushroom caps and pepper wedges.

5. Stir tempura batter until smooth. Dip 6 stuffed vegetables, 1 at a time, into batter. Carefully add to oil. Fry, stuffing sides up, about 2 minutes for peppers, 3 minutes for zucchini and 4 minutes for mushrooms or until golden brown, turning once. Remove vegetables to tray lined with paper towels; drain. Repeat with remaining stuffed vegetables, reheating oil between batches. Dip leftover unstuffed zucchini slices into remaining batter and fry about 3 minutes or until golden brown.

6. Serve immediately with favorite Asian dipping sauce.   *Makes 4 servings*

Fish & Chips

1. Combine flour, beer and 2 teaspoons oil in small bowl. Cover; refrigerate 1 to 2 hours.

2. Pour 2 inches oil into heavy skillet. Heat over medium heat until fresh bread cube placed in oil browns in 45 seconds (about 365°F). Add potato wedges in batches. (Do not crowd.) Fry potato wedges 4 to 6 minutes or until outsides are brown, turning once. Drain on paper towels; sprinkle lightly with salt. Repeat with remaining potato wedges. (Allow temperature of oil to return to 365°F between batches.) Reserve oil to fry cod.

3. Stir egg yolk into reserved flour mixture. Beat egg white in medium bowl with electric mixer at medium-high speed until soft peaks form. Fold egg white into flour mixture; set aside.

4. Rinse fish; pat dry with paper towels. Dip 4 fish pieces into batter; fry 4 to 6 minutes or until batter is crispy and brown and fish begins to flake when tested with fork, turning once. Drain on paper towels. Repeat with remaining fish pieces. (Allow temperature of oil to return to 365°F between batches.) Serve immediately with potato wedges. Serve with vinegar and lemon wedges, if desired.

Makes 4 servings

¾ cup all-purpose flour
½ cup flat beer or lemon-lime carbonated beverage
Vegetable oil for frying
4 medium russet potatoes, each cut into 8 wedges
Salt
1 egg, separated
1 pound cod fillets (about 6 to 8 small fillets)
Malt vinegar and lemon wedges (optional)

Deep-Fried Favorites

Fried Catfish with Cherry Salsa

Cherry Salsa
- **1 cup fresh sweet cherries, halved and pitted**
- **¼ cup red onion, minced**
- **1 medium jalapeño pepper, seeded and minced***
- **1 teaspoon balsamic vinegar**
- **½ teaspoon salt**
- **¹⁄₁₆ teaspoon allspice**

Fried Catfish
- **¼ cup flour**
- **2 tablespoons cornmeal**
- **¼ teaspoon salt**
- **¼ teaspoon black pepper**
- **¼ teaspoon paprika**
- **⅛ teaspoon garlic salt**
- **2 tablespoons vegetable oil**
- **4 medium catfish fillets (about 1¼ pounds)**
- **Lime wedges and chopped cilantro (optional)**

*Jalapeño peppers can sting and irritate the skin, so wear rubber gloves when handling peppers and do not touch your eyes.

1. For salsa, combine cherries, red onion, jalapeño, vinegar, ½ teaspoon salt and allspice in a bowl. Stir well and set aside.

2. For catfish, combine flour, cornmeal, ¼ teaspoon salt, pepper, paprika and garlic salt on a dinner plate. Heat oil in large heavy skillet. Dredge catfish in flour mixture, coating completely. Fry catfish over medium-high heat for 4 to 5 minutes per side or until fish is golden brown and opaque in center.

3. Serve catfish with cherry salsa. Garnish with lime wedges and cilantro, if desired.

Makes 4 servings

Dark Sweet Cherries

Crispy Tuna Fritters

1. Combine corn bread mix, onion, pimiento, salt, red pepper and black pepper in small bowl.

2. Slowly stir water into corn bread mixture. (Mixture will be thick.) Stir in tuna.

3. Pour oil into large skillet to depth of ½ inch; heat over medium heat until deep-fry thermometer registers about 375°F.

4. Drop corn bread mixture by tablespoonfuls into hot oil. Fry over medium heat 1 minute per side or until golden brown. Drain on paper towels.

Makes 6 servings (about 30 fritters)

Serving Suggestion: Serve fritters with cucumber ranch salad dressing or tartar sauce.

Prep and Cook Time: *30 minutes*

1 cup yellow corn
   bread mix
¼ cup minced onion
2 tablespoons minced
   pimiento
¼ teaspoon salt
⅛ teaspoon ground red
   pepper
⅛ teaspoon black pepper
¾ cup boiling water
1 can (9 ounces) tuna
   packed in water,
   drained
   Vegetable oil for frying

Coconut Fish Bites

1. Place coconut and peanuts in food processor. Process using on/off pulsing action until peanuts are ground, but not pasty.

2. Blend egg, soy sauce and salt in pie plate. Place cornstarch and coconut mixture on separate pieces of waxed paper.

3. Toss fish cubes in cornstarch until well coated. Add to egg mixture; toss until coated with egg mixture. Lightly coat with coconut mixture. Refrigerate until ready to cook.

4. Heat oil in heavy 3-quart saucepan over medium heat until deep-fry thermometer registers 365°F. Fry fish, in batches, 4 to 5 minutes or until golden brown and fish cubes begin to flake when tested with fork. Adjust heat to maintain temperature. (Allow oil to return to 365°F between batches.) Drain on paper towels. Serve with favorite Asian dipping Sauce. Garnish, if desired.

Makes about 24 appetizers

1 cup flaked coconut
½ cup unsalted peanuts
1 egg
1 tablespoon soy sauce
¼ teaspoon salt
⅓ cup cornstarch
1 pound firm white fish
   (orange roughy,
   haddock or cod fish),
   cut into 1-inch cubes
1 quart vegetable oil for
   frying
   Prepared Asian dipping
   sauce
   Lemon wedges and fresh
   celery leaves for
   garnish

Southern Fried Catfish with Hush Puppies

**Hush Puppy Batter
(recipe follows)
4 catfish fillets (about
1½ pounds)
½ cup yellow cornmeal
3 tablespoons all-purpose
flour
1½ teaspoons salt
¼ teaspoon ground red
pepper
Vegetable oil for frying
Fresh parsley sprigs for
garnish**

1. Prepare Hush Puppy Batter; set aside.

2. Rinse catfish; pat dry with paper towels. Combine cornmeal, flour, salt and red pepper in shallow dish. Dip fish into cornmeal mixture. Heat 1-inch oil in large heavy skillet over medium heat until deep-fry thermometer registers 375°F.

3. Fry fish in batches 4 to 5 minutes or until golden brown and fish begins to flake when tested with fork. (Allow temperature of oil to return to 375°F between batches.) Drain fish on paper towels.

4. To make Hush Puppies, drop batter by tablespoonfuls into hot oil. Fry, a few pieces at a time, 2 minutes or until golden brown. Garnish, if desired.

Makes 4 servings

Hush Puppy Batter

**1½ cups yellow cornmeal
½ cup all-purpose flour
2 teaspoons baking powder
½ teaspoon salt
1 cup milk
1 small onion, minced
1 egg, lightly beaten**

Combine cornmeal, flour, baking powder and salt in medium bowl. Add milk, onion and egg. Stir until well blended. Allow batter to stand 5 to 10 minutes before frying.

Makes about 24 hush puppies

Crab-Stuffed Shrimp

1. Heat 2 tablespoons oil in small saucepan over medium heat. Add onion; cook and stir until tender, about 3 minutes. Add curry powder; cook and stir 1 minute. Add 1½ tablespoons sherry, satay sauce, 2 teaspoons soy sauce and sugar; cook and stir 2 minutes. Stir in cream; bring to a boil. Simmer 2 minutes, stirring occasionally. Keep warm.

2. For shrimp, whisk egg whites, cornstarch, 1 tablespoon sherry and 1 tablespoon soy sauce in medium bowl. Add crabmeat, green onions and celery; mix well.

3. Cut deep slit into but not through back of each shrimp. Flatten shrimp slightly by pounding gently with mallet or rolling pin. Spoon crab mixture onto each shrimp, pressing into slit with back of spoon or small spatula. Coat each shrimp lightly with flour.

4. Beat eggs and milk with fork in shallow bowl until blended. Place each shrimp, stuffed-side up, in egg mixture, spooning egg mixture over shrimp to cover completely. Coat each shrimp with bread crumbs, pressing crumbs lightly onto shrimp. Place shrimp in single layer on cookie sheets or plates. Refrigerate 30 minutes.

5. Heat 1 inch of oil in wok or large skillet over high heat to 375°F. Add four or five shrimp at a time; cook until golden brown, about 3 minutes. Drain on paper towels. Serve with sauce.

Makes 4 servings

Sauce
- 2 tablespoons vegetable oil
- 1 small yellow onion, finely chopped
- 1 teaspoon curry powder
- 1½ tablespoons dry sherry
- 1 tablespoon satay sauce
- 2 teaspoons soy sauce
- 1 teaspoon sugar
- ¼ cup cream or milk

Shrimp
- 2 egg whites, lightly beaten
- 4 teaspoons cornstarch
- 1 tablespoon dry sherry
- 1 tablespoon soy sauce
- 2 cans (6½ ounces each) crabmeat, drained and flaked
- 8 green onions with tops, finely chopped
- 2 stalks celery, finely chopped
- 1½ pounds large raw shrimp, peeled and deveined
- ½ cup all-purpose flour
- 3 eggs
- 3 tablespoons milk
- 2 to 3 cups fresh bread crumbs (from 8 to 10 bread slices)
- Vegetable oil for frying

Batter-Fried Shark Bites

Pesto Mayonnaise (recipe follows)
1 pound shark steaks, about 1 inch thick
¾ cup all-purpose flour
½ teaspoon salt
¼ teaspoon baking powder
½ cup milk
1 egg, beaten
1 tablespoon butter, melted
Vegetable oil for frying

1. Prepare Pesto Mayonnaise.

2. Rinse shark and pat dry with paper towels. Remove skin from fish. Cut fish into 1-inch cubes. Place on paper towels; set aside.

3. Combine flour, salt and baking powder in shallow dish; make well in center. Add milk, egg and butter; beat until smooth. Heat 1 inch of oil in heavy deep skillet over medium heat to 365°F.

4. Dip 1 fish cube at a time into batter, coating all sides. Working in batches, place cubes into hot oil without crowding; fry until golden brown. Adjust heat to maintain temperature. (Allow temperature of oil to return to 365°F between each batch.)

5. Remove from skillet and drain on paper towels. Serve immediately with Pesto Mayonnaise. *Makes 30 appetizers*

Pesto Mayonnaise

½ cup mayonnaise
¼ cup prepared pesto
1 tablespoon lemon juice
Grated lemon peel for garnish

Combine mayonnaise, pesto and lemon juice in small bowl. Garnish, if desired. Refrigerate until ready to use. *Makes ¾ cup*

Fried Calamari with Tartar Sauce

1. Rinse squid under cold running water. Cut each squid body tube crosswise into ¼-inch rings. Pat rings and tentacles with paper towels until thoroughly dry.

2. Beat egg with milk in small bowl. Add squid pieces; stir to coat well. Spread bread crumbs on plate. Dip squid pieces in bread crumbs; place in shallow bowl or on waxed paper. Let stand 10 to 15 minutes before frying.

3. Heat 1½ inches oil in large saucepan to 350°F. (Caution: Squid will pop and spatter during frying; do not stand too close to pan.) Adjust heat to maintain temperature. Fry 8 to 10 pieces of squid at a time in hot oil 45 to 60 seconds until light brown. Remove with slotted spoon; drain on paper towels. Repeat with remaining squid pieces. *Do not overcook squid or it will become tough.* Serve hot with Tartar Sauce and lemon wedges. *Makes 2 to 3 servings*

Tartar Sauce

  1⅓ **cups mayonnaise**
    1 **green onion, thinly sliced**
    2 **tablespoons chopped fresh parsley**
    1 **tablespoon drained capers, minced**
    1 **small sweet gherkin or pickle, minced**

Combine all ingredients in small bowl; mix well. Cover and refrigerate until ready to serve. *Makes about 1⅓ cups*

1 **pound cleaned squid**
   (body tubes, tentacles
   or a combination)
1 **egg**
1 **tablespoon milk**
¾ **cup plain dry bread**
   crumbs
   Vegetable oil for frying
   Tartar Sauce (recipe
   follows)
   Lemon wedges

Deep-Fried Stuffed Shells

16 uncooked jumbo pasta
   shells
2 eggs, divided
1 can (6½ ounces) tuna,
   drained and flaked *or*
1 can (6 ounces)
   crabmeat, drained,
   flaked and cartilage
   removed
1 cup (4 ounces) shredded
   Cheddar cheese
1 medium tomato, peeled,
   seeded, and chopped
2 tablespoons sliced green
   onions
½ teaspoon dried basil
⅛ teaspoon black pepper
1 tablespoon water
1 cup dry bread crumbs
   Vegetable oil for frying
   Tomato sauce for dipping
   Crisp salad greens, carrot
   curls and dill sprigs for
   garnish

1. Cook shells according to package directions until tender but still firm; drain. Rinse under cold running water; drain again.

2. Invert shells on paper towel-lined plate to cool.

3. Lightly beat 1 egg in large bowl. Add tuna, cheese, tomato, green onions, basil and pepper; mix well. Using large spoon, stuff cooled shells with tuna mixture.

4. Beat remaining 1 egg with water in small bowl. Place bread crumbs in large, shallow dish. Dip each stuffed shell in egg mixture and roll in bread crumbs.

5. Heat 2 inches oil in large, heavy saucepan over medium-high heat until oil reaches 365°F; adjust heat to maintain temperature. Fry shells, a few at a time, in hot oil 1½ to 2 minutes until golden brown. Remove with slotted spoon; drain on paper towels. Serve with tomato sauce. Garnish, if desired.

Makes 8 servings

Crisp Fish Cakes

1. Process fish pieces in food processor 10 to 20 seconds or just until coarsely chopped. *Do not purée.* Add fish sauce, garlic, chopped cilantro, lemon peel, ginger and red pepper; process 5 seconds or until combined.

2. Rub cutting board with 1 to 2 teaspoons oil. Place fish mixture on board; pat evenly into 7-inch square. Cut into 16 squares; shape each square into 2-inch patty.

3. Heat 1 to 1½ inches oil in Dutch oven or large skillet over medium-high heat until oil registers 360°F to 375°F on deep-fry thermometer. Place 4 patties on slotted spoon and lower into hot oil.

4. Fry patties in batches 2 to 3 minutes or until golden and fish is opaque in center. (Do not crowd pan. Allow oil to return to temperature between batches.) Remove with slotted spoon to paper towels; drain.

5. To eat, place lettuce leaf on plate. Stack 1 fish cake, apple strips, cilantro and mint in center of lettuce leaf; fold to make packet.   *Makes 6 to 8 servings*

1 pound boneless catfish, halibut or cod fillets, cut into 1-inch pieces
1 tablespoon fish sauce
3 cloves garlic, minced
1 tablespoon chopped fresh cilantro
2 teaspoons grated lemon peel
1 teaspoon finely chopped fresh ginger
⅛ teaspoon ground red pepper
Peanut oil for frying
1 head curly leaf lettuce
1 medium green or red apple, cut into thin strips
½ cup fresh cilantro leaves
⅓ cup fresh mint leaves

Light Choices

Beijing Fillet of Sole

2 tablespoons soy sauce

2 teaspoons dark
    sesame oil

4 sole fillets (6 ounces
    each)

1¼ cups coleslaw mix or
    shredded cabbage

½ cup crushed chow mein
    noodles

1 egg white, lightly beaten

2 teaspoons sesame seeds

1 package (10 ounces)
    frozen snow peas,
    cooked and drained

1. Preheat oven to 350°F. Combine soy sauce and oil in small bowl. Place sole in shallow dish. Lightly brush both sides of sole with soy sauce mixture.

2. Combine cabbage, noodles, egg white and remaining soy sauce mixture in medium bowl. Spoon evenly over each fillet. Roll up fillets. Place, seam side down, in shallow foil-lined roasting pan.

3. Sprinkle rolls with sesame seeds. Bake 25 to 30 minutes or until fish begins to flake when tested with fork. Serve with snow peas. *Makes 4 servings*

Buttery Pepper and Citrus Broiled Fish

3 tablespoons MOLLY
    MCBUTTER® Flavored
    Sprinkles
1 tablespoon MRS. DASH®
    Lemon Pepper Blend
1 tablespoon lime juice
2 teaspoons honey
1 pound boneless white
    fish fillets

Combine first 4 ingredients in small bowl; mix well. Broil fish 6 to 8 inches from heat, about 5 minutes, turning once. Spread with Lemon Pepper mixture. Broil an additional 4 to 5 minutes.

Makes 4 servings

Prep and Cook Time: *15 minutes*

Crab Louis Stuffed Tomatoes

Cut tomatoes in half crosswise. Push out and discard seeds with your finger. Use a small knife to cut out pulp from each tomato half leaving shells intact. Chop pulp; transfer to a bowl and stir in sour cream, ketchup, chives and horseradish. Stir in crabmeat; spoon mixture into tomato shells. Serve on lettuce lined plates.

Makes 2 servings

2 large ripe tomatoes
3 tablespoons reduced-fat sour cream
3 tablespoons ketchup or chili sauce
2 tablespoons chopped chives or green onion tops
1 teaspoon prepared horseradish
8 ounces imitation crabmeat, shredded (read labels for brands with lowest sodium)
2 large Boston or red leaf lettuce leaves

Herbed Shrimp and Mushrooms with Fettuccine

6 ounces uncooked spinach fettuccine
4 teaspoons olive oil
2 cups sliced mushrooms
½ cup chopped onion
1 to 2 cloves garlic, minced
⅓ cup fat-free reduced-sodium chicken broth
⅓ cup dry white wine
2 teaspoons cornstarch
½ teaspoon dried rosemary
¼ teaspoon salt
¼ teaspoon black pepper
1 pound large raw shrimp, peeled and deveined
1 large tomato, seeded and chopped
¼ cup slivered fresh basil leaves
¼ cup finely shredded Asiago or Parmesan cheese

1. Cook pasta according to package directions, omitting salt and fat. Drain and keep warm.

2. Heat oil in large skillet over medium heat. Add mushrooms, onion and garlic; cook and stir 5 minutes or until onion is tender.

3. Combine broth, wine, cornstarch, rosemary, salt and pepper in small bowl; stir until smooth. Add to mushroom mixture. Bring to a boil, stirring constantly. Add shrimp; return to a boil. Reduce heat; simmer, covered, 1 to 3 minutes or just until shrimp are pink and opaque. Stir in tomato and basil.

4. Toss shrimp mixture with pasta. Sprinkle with cheese.   *Makes 6 servings*

Prep Time: *20 minutes*
Cook Time: *10 minutes*

Southwest Roasted Salmon & Corn

1. Preheat oven to 400°F. Spray shallow 1-quart baking dish with nonstick cooking spray. Pull back husks from each ear of corn, leaving husks attached. Discard silk. Bring husks back up over each ear. Soak corn in cold water 20 minutes.

2. Place salmon, skin side down, in prepared dish. Drizzle 1 tablespoon lime juice over fillets. Marinate at room temperature 15 minutes.

3. Combine garlic, chili powder, cumin, oregano, half of salt and pepper in small bowl. Pat salmon lightly with paper towel. Rub garlic mixture on tops and sides of salmon.

4. Remove corn from water. Place corn on one side of oven rack. Roast 10 minutes; turn.

5. Place salmon in baking dish on other side of oven rack. Roast 15 minutes or until salmon is opaque in center, and corn is tender.

6. Combine margarine, cilantro, remaining 1 teaspoon lime juice and remaining salt in small bowl. Remove husks from corn. Brush over corn. Serve corn with salmon. *Makes 2 servings*

Recipe Tip: Roasting corn gives it a special flavor. However, it can also be cooked in boiling water. Omit steps 1 and 4. Husk corn and place in large pot of boiling water. Cover; remove from heat and let stand for 10 minutes. Drain and brush with cilantro mixture as directed.

2 medium ears fresh corn, unhusked
1 salmon fillet (6 ounces), cut into 2 equal pieces
1 tablespoon plus 1 teaspoon fresh lime juice, divided
1 clove garlic, minced
½ teaspoon chili powder
¼ teaspoon ground cumin
¼ teaspoon dried oregano
⅛ teaspoon salt, divided
⅛ teaspoon black pepper
2 teaspoons margarine, melted
2 teaspoons minced fresh cilantro

Rosemary-Garlic Scallops with Polenta

2 teaspoons olive oil
1 red bell pepper, seeded and sliced
⅓ cup chopped red onion
3 cloves garlic, minced
8 ounces fresh bay scallops
2 teaspoons chopped fresh rosemary leaves or ¾ teaspoon dried rosemary
¼ teaspoon black pepper
1¼ cups fat-free reduced-sodium chicken broth
½ cup cornmeal
¼ teaspoon salt

1. Heat oil in large nonstick skillet over medium heat. Add bell pepper, onion and garlic. Cook for 5 minutes. Add scallops, rosemary and black pepper. Cook until scallops are opaque, 3 to 5 minutes, stirring occasionally.

2. Meanwhile, combine broth, cornmeal and salt in small saucepan. Bring to a boil over high heat. Reduce heat to low and simmer for 5 minutes or until polenta is very thick, stirring frequently. Transfer to two serving plates. Top polenta with scallop mixture.

Makes 2 servings

Light Choices

Grilled Fish with Buttery Lemon Parsley

1. Preheat grill to medium-high heat. Coat cold grid with cooking spray; place over heat.

2. Combine margarine, parsley, lemon peel, salt and rosemary in small bowl; set aside.

3. Coat fish with cooking spray; place on grid. Grill, uncovered, 3 minutes. Turn; grill 2 to 3 minutes longer or until opaque in center.

4. To serve, squeeze juice from 1 lemon half evenly over each fillet. Top with equal amounts of parsley mixture.

Makes 6 servings

Nonstick cooking spray
6 tablespoons margarine
3 tablespoons finely chopped fresh parsley
1 teaspoon grated lemon peel
½ teaspoon salt
½ teaspoon dried rosemary
6 fish fillets (6 ounces each), such as grouper, snapper or any lean white fish
3 medium lemons, halved

Light Choices

Caribbean Sea Bass with Mango Salsa

4 skinless sea bass fillets
  (4 ounces each), about
  1 inch thick
1 teaspoon Caribbean jerk
  seasoning
  Nonstick cooking spray
1 ripe mango, peeled and
  diced, *or* 1 cup diced
  drained bottled mango
2 tablespoons chopped
  fresh cilantro
2 teaspoons fresh lime
  juice
1 teaspoon minced fresh or
  bottled jalapeño
  pepper*

*Jalapeño peppers can sting and
irritate the skin, so wear rubber gloves
when handling peppers and do not
touch your eyes.*

1. Prepare grill or preheat broiler. Sprinkle fish with seasoning; coat lightly with cooking spray. Grill fish over medium coals or broil 5 inches from heat 4 to 5 minutes per side or until fish begins to flake when tested with fork.

2. Meanwhile, combine mango, cilantro, lime juice and jalapeño in small bowl; mix well. Serve salsa over fish. *Makes 4 servings*

Prep Time: *10 minutes*
Cook Time: *8 minutes*

Halibut Provençale

1. Place an ovenproof 12-inch skillet over medium heat and coat with cooking spray. Add tomatoes, fennel, onion, orange peel and herbes de Provence. Cook 10 minutes, stirring often.

2. Place halibut over vegetables; sprinkle with oil. Mix bread crumbs, cheese, garlic, paprika, pepper and salt together. Sprinkle over fish. Cover skillet and cook until fish begins to flake.

3. Alternatively, heat broiler. Place skillet under broiler until bread crumbs are golden brown, 1 to 2 minutes. Sprinkle fish with minced basil, if desired.

Makes 4 servings

Note: Herbes de Provence is an herb blend that usually contains dried basil, fennel seed, lavender, marjoram, rosemary, sage, summer savory, and thyme.

Nonstick cooking spray
1 can (28 ounces) diced tomatoes
2 cups fennel, stems and fronds removed, sliced thin and chopped
1 cup finely chopped onion
2 tablespoons grated orange peel
2 teaspoons dried herbes de Provence
4 halibut steaks (4 ounces each)
1 tablespoon olive oil

Topping
¼ cup plain dry bread crumbs
1 tablespoon Parmesan cheese, grated
2 cloves garlic, minced
1 teaspoon paprika
½ teaspoon black pepper
¼ teaspoon salt
Minced fresh basil (optional)

Light Choices

Fast Catfish in Foil

4 catfish fillets (4 ounces each)
2 cups shredded carrots
6 ounces green beans, ends trimmed (about 60 beans)
8 unpeeled baby red potatoes
  Nonstick cooking spray
4 teaspoons lemon juice
2 teaspoons dried parsley
1 teaspoon black pepper

1. Preheat oven to 425°F. Place one fillet, skin side down, on each of 4 (12×12-inch) sheets of aluminum foil. Top each fillet with ½ cup shredded carrots, green beans and potato quarters.

2. Spray ingredients on each foil square with cooking spray. Sprinkle with 1 teaspoon lemon juice, ½ teaspoon parsley and ¼ teaspoon pepper.

3. Fold foil into packets, sealing securely. Place packets on baking sheet; bake 30 minutes.

4. Remove packets from oven; let stand 5 minutes. Carefully open packets allowing steam to escape. Serve immediately. *Makes 4 servings*

Tuna Steaks with Tomatoes & Olives

2 teaspoons olive oil
1 small onion, quartered and sliced
1 clove garlic, minced
1⅓ cups chopped tomatoes
¼ cup sliced pitted black olives
2 anchovy fillets, finely chopped (optional)
2 tablespoons chopped fresh basil
¼ teaspoon salt, divided
⅛ teaspoon red pepper flakes
4 tuna steaks (¾ inch thick)
  Black pepper
  Nonstick cooking spray
¼ cup toasted pine nuts (optional)

1. Heat oil in large skillet over medium heat. Add onion; cook and stir 4 minutes. Add garlic; cook and stir about 30 seconds. Add tomatoes; cook 3 minutes, stirring occasionally. Stir in olives, anchovy fillets, if desired, basil, ⅛ teaspoon salt and pepper flakes. Cook until hot and most of liquid had evaporated.

2. Meanwhile, sprinkle tuna with remaining ⅛ teaspoon salt and black pepper. Spray large nonstick skillet with cooking spray. Heat over medium high heat. Cook tuna 2 minutes per side or until tuna is medium-rare or to desired doneness. Serve with tomato mixture. Garnish with pine nuts, if desired.

Scallops and Marinara Sauce on Spinach Fettuccine

1. For Marinara Sauce, heat 1 teaspoon olive oil in saucepan over medium heat. Add onion. Cook and stir 3 minutes or until onion is soft. Add mushrooms, pepper, tomatoes and chili paste, if desired. Bring to a boil over high heat. Reduce heat to low. Cover and simmer 15 minutes, stirring occasionally.

2. Cook fettuccine according to package directions, omitting salt. Drain; keep warm. Meanwhile, heat remaining 2 teaspoons olive oil in large nonstick skillet over medium heat. Add scallops. Cook and stir 4 minutes or until scallops are opaque.

3. Divide spinach fettuccine among serving plates. Top with marinara sauce and scallops. Sprinkle with Parmesan and chives. *Makes 4 servings*

Prep and Cook Time: *30 minutes*

3 teaspoons olive oil, divided
1 cup chopped onion
1 cup sliced mushrooms
1 red bell pepper, chopped
1 can (about 14 ounces) Italian-style stewed tomatoes, undrained
½ teaspoon Thai chili paste* (optional)
9 ounces fresh uncooked spinach fettuccine
12 ounces scallops, rinsed and drained
2 tablespoons freshly grated Parmesan cheese
2 teaspoons chopped chives

*Thai chili paste is available at some larger supermarkets and at Oriental markets.

·145·
Light Choices

Lemoned Shrimp with Basil

Nonstick cooking spray
1 pound medium raw shrimp, peeled and deveined
4 cloves garlic, minced
1 teaspoon grated lemon peel
¼ teaspoon seafood seasoning mix
¼ teaspoon red pepper flakes
2 tablespoons margarine
2 tablespoons lemon juice
2 tablespoons chopped fresh basil

1. Coat a 12-inch nonstick skillet with cooking spray and heat over medium heat. Add shrimp, garlic, lemon peel, seafood seasoning and red pepper flakes. Cook 4 minutes or until shrimp are pink and opaque, stirring frequently.

2. Remove from heat; add remaining ingredients. Serve in individual baking dishes or ramekins.

Makes 4 servings

Serving Suggestion: Serve with cooked brown rice and steamed asparagus spears.

Curried Fish Casserole

1. Preheat oven to 350°F. Spray 13×9-inch baking dish with cooking spray. Add bok choy, ½ cup bell pepper, rice and ⅓ cup water; toss gently to blend.

2. Arrange fillets over vegetables; sprinkle with ¼ teaspoon salt. Cover with foil; bake 20 minutes or until fish begins to flake when tested with fork.

3. Meanwhile, combine broth, remaining ½ cup bell pepper, curry powder, sugar and remaining ¼ teaspoon salt in small saucepan. Bring to a boil over medium-high heat. Cook and stir 1 minute.

4. Combine cornstarch and remaining 3 tablespoons water in small bowl; stir until completely dissolved. Add to curry mixture; cook and stir 1 minute, scraping bottom and side of pan to prevent sticking.

5. Serve fish fillets over rice and vegetable mixture. Spoon sauce over top. Garnish with green onions, if desired.

Makes 4 servings

Nonstick cooking spray
2 cups thinly sliced bok choy or napa cabbage
1 cup sliced red bell pepper, divided
½ cup uncooked quick-cooking brown rice
⅓ cup plus 3 tablespoons water, divided
4 Tilapia or white fish fillets (¼ pound each)
½ teaspoon salt, divided
1 cup fat-free reduced-sodium chicken broth
1 teaspoon curry powder
¾ teaspoon sugar
1 tablespoon cornstarch
¼ cup finely chopped green onions (optional)

Curry Powder

Light Choices

Chilean Sea Bass Veracruz

¾ pound Chilean sea bass steaks or halibut steaks, skinned, boned and cut into 1-inch cubes

3 tablespoons lime juice, divided

⅛ teaspoon black pepper

4 large tomatoes, seeded and diced

1 large onion, diced

3 cloves garlic, finely minced

2 to 3 serrano peppers,* seeded and finely chopped

Olive oil cooking spray

2 tablespoons chopped fresh cilantro

3 cups hot cooked rice

Serrano peppers can sting and irritate the skin, so wear rubber gloves when handling peppers and do not touch your eyes.

1. Place fish, 1 tablespoon lime juice and black pepper in small bowl. Stir well and let marinate at least 15 minutes, but not more than 30 minutes.

2. Meanwhile, combine tomatoes, onion and garlic in medium bowl. Stir in serrano peppers; mix well.

3. Spray medium nonstick skillet with cooking spray; heat over high heat. Add fish; cook and stir 2 to 3 minutes or until lightly browned. Reduce heat to medium; cover and cook about 5 minutes, stirring occasionally, or until fish just begins to flake. Remove fish to clean bowl; set aside.

4. Return skillet to medium heat; add tomato mixture. Cook and stir about 3 minutes or just until onions are soft. Return fish to skillet; cook and stir 2 minutes. Remove from heat. Add remaining 2 tablespoons lime juice and cilantro. Serve over rice.

Makes 4 servings

Light Choices

Tilapia & Sweet Corn Baked in Parchment

1. Preheat oven to 400°F. Cut two 15-inch squares of parchment paper; fold each piece in half.

2. Combine corn, onion, bell pepper, garlic, ½ teaspoon fresh rosemary, ¼ teaspoon salt and half the black pepper in small bowl. Open parchment paper; spoon half the corn mixture on one side of each piece, spreading out slightly.

3. Arrange tilapia fillets on top of corn mixture. Brush fish with oil; sprinkle with remaining ½ teaspoon fresh rosemary, ¼ teaspoon salt and black pepper.

4. To seal packets, fold other half of parchment over fish and corn. Fold and crimp along edges until completely sealed. Place packets on baking sheet.

5. Bake 15 minutes or until fish is opaque in center. Remove packets to serving plates. Carefully cut centers of packets and peel back paper.

Makes 2 servings

Note: Heavy-duty foil can be substituted for the parchment paper. To serve, remove fish and corn from foil.

⅔ cup fresh or frozen corn kernels
¼ cup finely chopped onion
¼ cup finely chopped red bell pepper
2 cloves garlic, minced
1 teaspoon chopped fresh rosemary leaves *or* ½ teaspoon dried rosemary, divided
½ teaspoon salt, divided
¼ to ½ teaspoon black pepper, divided
2 tilapia fillets (4 ounces each)
1 teaspoon olive oil

Vermouth Salmon

2 (10×10-inch) sheets
heavy-duty foil
2 salmon fillets or steaks
(3 ounces each)
Salt and black pepper
4 sprigs fresh dill
2 slices lemon
1 tablespoon vermouth

1. Preheat oven to 375°F. Turn up edges of 1 sheet of foil so juices will not run out. Place salmon in center of foil. Sprinkle with salt and pepper. Place dill and lemon slices on top of salmon. Pour vermouth evenly over fish pieces.

2. Cover fish with second sheet of foil. Crimp edges of foil together to seal packet, leaving some space for heat circulation. Place packet on baking sheet. Bake 20 to 25 minutes or until salmon begins to flake when tested with fork.

Makes 2 servings

Light Choices

Broiled Scallops with Honey-Lime Marinade

Combine honey, lime juice, oil, lime peel, salt and hot pepper sauce in large bowl. Rinse scallops and pat dry with paper towel; add to marinade. Marinate scallops in refrigerator, stirring occasionally 1 hour or overnight. Preheat broiler. Arrange scallops and marinade in single layer in 2 individual broiler-proof dishes. Broil 4 inches from heat source 4 to 7 minutes or until opaque and lightly browned. Serve with lime wedges. *Makes 2 servings*

Favorite recipe from **National Honey Board**

2 tablespoons honey
4 teaspoons lime juice
1 tablespoon vegetable oil
¼ teaspoon grated lime peel
¼ teaspoon salt
1 dash hot pepper sauce
½ pound bay, calico or sea scallops
1 lime, cut into wedges

Hoppin' Shrimp and Brown Rice

1 bag boil-in-bag instant
   brown rice
   Nonstick cooking spray
12 ounces (72 shrimp or
   about ¾ cup) frozen
   cooked baby shrimp
1 can (about 14 ounces)
   no-salt-added diced
   tomatoes
1 box (10 ounces) frozen
   whole okra
2 cups frozen black-eyed
   peas
2 cups reduced-fat
   low-sodium vegetable
   broth
2 cups bottled salsa with
   jalapeños
4 stalks celery, trimmed
   and chopped
¼ cup chopped red onion
¼ cup chopped fresh
   cilantro
½ teaspoon black pepper
   Juice of ½ lime
   Lime Wedges (optional)

1. Prepare rice according to package directions, omitting any fat or salt.

2. Lightly coat deep skillet with cooking spray. Add shrimp, tomatoes, okra, black-eyed peas, broth, salsa, celery, onion, cilantro, black pepper and lime juice. Cook on high for 20 minutes, stirring occasionally.

3. Place ½ cup rice in large soup bowl, top with 1½ cups shrimp mixture, garnish with additional salsa, cilantro and lime wedges, if desired.

Makes 4 servings

Light Choices

Skillet Fish with Lemon Tarragon "Butter"

1. Combine margarine, 2 teaspoons lemon juice, lemon peel, mustard, tarragon and salt in small bowl. Blend well with fork; set aside.

2. Coat 12-inch nonstick skillet with cooking spray. Heat over medium heat.

3. Drizzle fillets with remaining 2 teaspoons lemon juice. Sprinkle one side of each fillet with paprika. Place fillets in skillet, paprika side down; cook 3 minutes. Gently turn and cook 3 minutes longer or until fish begins to flake when tested with fork. Place fillets on serving plates; top with margarine mixture.   *Makes 2 servings*

2 teaspoons margarine
4 teaspoons lemon juice, divided
½ teaspoon grated lemon peel
¼ teaspoon prepared mustard
¼ teaspoon dried tarragon
⅛ teaspoon salt
   Nonstick cooking spray
2 lean white fish fillets (4 ounces each),* rinsed and patted dry
¼ teaspoon paprika

Cod, orange roughy, flounder, haddock, halibut or sole can be used.

Light Choices

Acknowledgments

The publisher would like to thank the companies listed below
for the use of their recipes in this publication.

Birds Eye Foods

California Olive Industry

Chef Paul Prudhomme's Magic Seasoning Blends®

Del Monte Corporation

Florida Department of Agriculture and Consumer Services,
Bureau of Seafood and Aquaculture

Grandma's® is a registered trademark of Mott's, LLP

The Hidden Valley® Food Products Company

MASTERFOODS USA

Mrs. Dash®

National Fisheries Institute

National Honey Board

Ortega®, A Division of B&G Foods, Inc.

Reckitt Benckiser Inc.

StarKist® Tuna

Reprinted with permission of Sunkist Growers, Inc. All Rights Reserved.

Unilever

Index

Index

Metric Conversion Chart

VOLUME MEASUREMENTS (dry)

⅛ teaspoon = 0.5 mL
¼ teaspoon = 1 mL
½ teaspoon = 2 mL
¾ teaspoon = 4 mL
1 teaspoon = 5 mL
1 tablespoon = 15 mL
2 tablespoons = 30 mL
¼ cup = 60 mL
⅓ cup = 75 mL
½ cup = 125 mL
⅔ cup = 150 mL
¾ cup = 175 mL
1 cup = 250 mL
2 cups = 1 pint = 500 mL
3 cups = 750 mL
4 cups = 1 quart = 1 L

VOLUME MEASUREMENTS (fluid)

1 fluid ounce (2 tablespoons) = 30 mL
4 fluid ounces (½ cup) = 125 mL
8 fluid ounces (1 cup) = 250 mL
12 fluid ounces (1½ cups) = 375 mL
16 fluid ounces (2 cups) = 500 mL

WEIGHTS (mass)

½ ounce = 15 g
1 ounce = 30 g
3 ounces = 90 g
4 ounces = 120 g
8 ounces = 225 g
10 ounces = 285 g
12 ounces = 360 g
16 ounces = 1 pound = 450 g

DIMENSIONS

1/16 inch = 2 mm
⅛ inch = 3 mm
¼ inch = 6 mm
½ inch = 1.5 cm
¾ inch = 2 cm
1 inch = 2.5 cm

OVEN TEMPERATURES

250°F = 120°C
275°F = 140°C
300°F = 150°C
325°F = 160°C
350°F = 180°C
375°F = 190°C
400°F = 200°C
425°F = 220°C
450°F = 230°C

BAKING PAN SIZES

Utensil	Size in Inches/Quarts	Metric Volume	Size in Centimeters
Baking or Cake Pan (square or rectangular)	8×8×2	2 L	20×20×5
	9×9×2	2.5 L	23×23×5
	12×8×2	3 L	30×20×5
	13×9×2	3.5 L	33×23×5
Loaf Pan	8×4×3	1.5 L	20×10×7
	9×5×3	2 L	23×13×7
Round Layer Cake Pan	8×1½	1.2 L	20×4
	9×1½	1.5 L	23×4
Pie Plate	8×1¼	750 mL	20×3
	9×1¼	1 L	23×3
Baking Dish or Casserole	1 quart	1 L	—
	1½ quart	1.5 L	—
	2 quart	2 L	—